God on the Open Road

on the

Steve Chapman

HARVEST HOUSE PUBLISHERS
Eugene, Oregon 97402

Cover by Paz Design Group, Salem, Oregon

WITH GOD ON THE OPEN ROAD
Copyright © 2002 by Steve Chapman
Published by Harvest House Publishers
Eugene, Oregon 97402

ISBN: 0-7369-0910-9

Printed in the United States of America.

02 03 04 05 06 07 08 09 10 / BP-MS / 10 9 8 7 6 5 4 3 2 1

To my wife, Annie,
for the constant companionship she
has given me on this ride through life.

Contents

A Note from Steve

Many times God has touched my heart with insights about Himself when the noise level around me was at its loudest. I have discovered numerous truths of Scripture while reading His Word sitting in a window seat at the back of a plane next to a powerful jet engine. Perhaps it's because absolutely nothing else can be heard but the Spirit of God. Riding lawn mowers also provide a significant amount of decibels to accomplish the same thing. In *A Look at Life from a Deer Stand*, I share how God even speaks quietly to a person's heart while he or she is hunting next to an incredibly busy interstate highway.

One other noisy time and place where the Lord has softly spoken to my heart is while my head is inside my full-face motorcycle helmet. As the wind creates that familiar, continuous roar around my noggin, all other audible distractions are eliminated. Taking advantage of these times to "chew on a piece of the Bread of Life" (God's Word) has yielded true nourishment and joy to my soul.

To help you experience this spiritual closeness with God, I've included a brief portion of Scripture at the end of each devotion. It not only highlights the subject but is also concise enough to quickly memorize.

As you prepare to ride, may I suggest that you reread the Scripture for the day. Then, as you hit the open road, you can pray over the passage, ponder it, and present your mind and heart to the Lord to hear His insights. Ride carefully and listen intently!

Iron Art

My wife, Annie, asked me a question one day that I couldn't immediately answer. "Just what is it about motor-cycles that you like?" I didn't want to respond with a sur-face reply like "they're fun"! She deserved more than the simple truth. Her tone of concern warned me that I needed to offer her something of substance. I needed to give her a well-thought-out answer that provided the deeper reasons I was drawn to a world that has certain risks and was foreign to her. After giving it some serious consideration, here's my answer to her question. There are five reasons motorcycles and motorcycling intrigue me. Here they are in reverse order of importance.

1. I enjoy looking at "iron" art. In the manner that some folks can stare at and admire a classic Rembrandt painting or a Michelangelo sculpture, I can gawk at a bike. I've been known to go to cycle shops merely to walk the showroom floor and feast my eyes on the machines. Just to look at the way form and function are married on two wheels is pure recreation. How the pipes softly turn and caress the frame in order to make room for human legs is a treat to behold. How the handlebars sweep back (on many models) as if to say, "Let's hold hands and have some fellowship in the wind," is sweet to imagine. It's art, and I'm a fan.

2. Another reason I am drawn to bikes is the thrill of the ride. The best way I can explain it is that mounting a motorcycle and heading out onto the road can make a trip to the IRS office seem like fun. (The arrival is another matter!) Acceleration, balance, shifting, leaning, turning, the wind, the openness are some of the ingredients that go into making the salve that treats the rash called "mundane."

3. There's the practicality of a bike that I like, too. My nimble number can go the 12 miles to town to do business a lot cheaper, by far, than my V-8 pickup. Parking is a breeze, too!

4. Then there's the people. The biking community is a special collection of close-knit individuals who I enjoy being around. Whenever one person finds out another is a saddle hugger, even if he or she is a stranger, there is an immediate bond between the two of them. It's instant friendship and fellowship.

5. Finally, my favorite part of owning and operating a motorcycle is the sabbaticals it offers. I've been told all my life that getting alone with God from time to time is as important to my spirit as breathing is to my flesh. This being true, I am always in need of those times when I'm alone in His presence. It is in those moments that He whispers His words to my heart to teach me, to listen to me, and to let me commune with Him. On an open road is a wonderful place to tune my heart to God.

These five reasons for being attracted to motorcycles satisfied Annie. I believe that the one she appreciates the most is the way the Lord uses the motorcycle as a tool to reveal His truths to me. Many of those insights are the contents of the pages that follow. They have come either while riding, planning to ride, or just pondering something seen while cruising down the road. It is my hope that these offerings will inspire you to begin (or restart) your own journal of what God has taught you through the unique world of motorcycling.

Blessed art You, O LORD!
Teach me Your statutes!

Psalm 119:12 NKJV

1

The Wave Offering

And the blood of Jesus His Son
cleanses us from all sin.
1 John 1:7

There is a unique and silent exchange that often takes place when two bikers pass on the open highway. It is anticipated with a quiet joy. The moment that familiar, lone headlight is seen dancing in the distance each individual makes his or her plan to participate in the deal. It's a ritual not common among drivers of vehicles with more than two or three wheels. And it is not a thing that normally happens between folks who are more than likely complete strangers.

The exchange happens as the machines near their passing point. The left hand of each rider carefully lets go of their handlebar and briefly waves, usually with the index finger pointing horizontal to the pavement. In that passing moment, though not a word is uttered, so much is said: "I'm one of you. We are mysteriously connected. Our wheels may be rolling in opposite directions, but our hearts fly side by side. I'm glad there is another like me out here. I'm glad we met. Be safe!"

Borrowing an ancient phrase from Leviticus 10:15, this momentary trade among passing motorcyclists could be called a "wave offering." In no way, of course, could this gesture between two riders ever match the meaning of the original "wave offering," but at least it could be a worthy reminder of an activity that had incredible significance in ages past.

As stated in the biblical record, the wave offering was one among many types of sacrifices that were made by the people of Israel. The sin and trespass offerings, for example, were done first by the worshiper to ensure pardon from God and establish communion with Him. Other sacrifices such as burnt offerings, peace offerings, and thank offerings were made after being admitted into a state of grace. Some of these rituals would last for days, and they were not only bloody due to the killing of animals but also very detailed in the manner the slaughters were carried out. There was nothing simple about it.

Thankfully, the ultimate sacrifice for sin was made once and for all at the cross of Christ. Hebrews 9:11-12 holds the "Good News" about this final and forever source of cleansing from our transgressions:

> But when Christ appeared as a high priest of the good things to come, He entered through the greater and more perfect tabernacle, not made with hands, that is to say, not of this creation; and not through the blood of goats and calves, but through His own blood, He entered the holy place once for all, having obtained eternal redemption.

Today, when you roll down the highway and see the approaching headlight glow of another bike, allow two things to happen. As your left hand cautiously slips off the bar and you point toward the passing stranger, let the fellowship of the "wave offering" remind you that because of the sacrifice Christ made, no other offering for sin is needed. Second, pray for the passing rider that he or she

will come to know the truth that has changed your life—
"we have been sanctified through the offering of the body
of Jesus Christ once for all" (Hebrews 10:10).

*Thank You, Jesus, for the sacrifice You made by offering Your
body and blood for the redemption and salvation of my soul. I
am eternally grateful. May my wave offerings on the highway
always remind me of Your boundless love toward me. Help me
to never fail to pass it on to others. In Your name I pray,
amen.*

He Himself is the propitiation for our sins;
and not for ours only, but also for
those of the whole world.

1 John 2:2

2

You'll Shoot Your Eye Out

*Bless the LORD, O my soul...who satisfies
your years with good things.*

Psalm 103:1,5

In the movie *A Christmas Story*, the featured character is a young boy named Ralphie who desperately desires to see a specific gift under the tree. Over and over, his fantasies of owning a "Red Rider Carbine Action Two Hundred Shot Lightning Loader Range Model BB gun...with a compass in the stock and a thing which tells time" are deflated by his mother's fear. Her highly emotional response to his relentless hints is a disappointing, "You'll shoot your eye out!"

Several years ago, when our family first viewed the film, the mother's line became famous in our home. Much to our kids' regret, it was parentally used with some disturbing regularity. Fortunately for them, they were into their teens when the movie came along, and items such as my high-powered rifle and a set of golf clubs had already been in their hands. (I mention the golf clubs because the scar on my face testifies to what can happen when children are around!). We used the phrase in reference to the use of some other potentially harmful devices and activities.

When our son, Nathan, was a teenager, for example, he started hinting that he would like to take flying lessons at a local airport. We said, "You'll shoot your eye out!" He knew exactly what we meant. "Forget it! We don't want to find you strewn in pieces around the nearby cornfields!" When our daughter, Heidi, was 16 and newly licensed to drive, she wanted to motor across the state to see her friend. We said, "You'll shoot your eye out!"

To be honest, even as a self-proclaimed, rugged, "outdoorsy" kind of dad, I managed to squelch my share of adventures by sowing the seeds of fear (I prefer to use the word *respect*) for certain things my kids wanted to experience. But be sure, what one sows, one will reap. Enter... the motorcycle.

For years my dream of straddling a motor entertained my psyche. When I finally brought the subject up in my mid-forties era, sadly enough what did I hear when I mentioned the motorcycle? You're exactly correct. "You'll shoot your eye out!" came at me with deserved accuracy. However, I had a well-thought-out, two-tiered argument for the purchase of an iron horse.

One, I had reached the season of my life when speed no longer tempted me. I assured my youngins that safety was of the utmost importance to me. Second, the incredibly high gas prices at the time merited the introduction of a non-gas-guzzling vehicle to use for local trips to the town where we conducted bank and postal business. Money savings was a viable issue. Even with such justifiable defenses for a bike, the looks of doubt on the faces of my children (and their mother) told me they were still apprehensive!

As it turned out, time and a necessary sense of caution yielded some accomplishments. Nathan has had some firsthand experience at the controls of an airplane, Heidi has driven across most of the state, and I...I have a motorcycle! To date, the three of us still have two eyes each. (Annie has nervously plucked hers out—no, not really.)

Perhaps the best yield from our risky adventures is that we have become better students of a passage found in Philippians 4:8:

> Finally, brethren, whatever is true, whatever is honorable, whatever is right, whatever is pure, whatever is lovely, whatever is of good repute, if there is any excellence and if anything worthy of praise, dwell on these things.

While most of life is sort of like riding a motorcycle in that it has constant and inherent dangers, we cannot dwell on the dark side of things and expect light to come through the windows. One of the reasons I truly enjoy the community of motorcyclists is that most of the people, if not all, are consummate optimists. More times than they want they hear this warning in one way or another: "You'll shoot your eye out!" Yet they smile, and the gleam on their faces says, "Lovely day for a ride." These folks are not blind to the hazards; they simply choose to look past them. For me, that brand of positive confidence is inspiring. I am proud to be among their number!

Father in heaven, thank You for supplying my years with good things, including the ability to look at the bright side. Help me see it more often. Thank You also for the adventures of this life that teach me to focus on the pure and the lovely. I pray for Your grace and mercy as I daily learn to keep looking to You. In Jesus' name, amen.

**Practice these things,
and the God of peace will be with you.**

Philippians 4:9

3

Holy Hankering

Then we who are alive and remain shall be caught up together with them in the clouds to meet the Lord in the air. And thus we shall always be with the Lord.

1 Thessalonians 4:17 NKJV

The word "hankering" was often used when I was growing up in West Virginia, but I rarely hear it these days. I personally like to use it because it describes so well a feeling I get from time to time, especially as a motorcyclist. While the origin of the word is a mystery to me (some say it has Dutch roots), its meaning may be best explained by the following scenario:

> Let's say the weather is remarkable. It's dry, sunny, and about 75 degrees. Somewhere deep inside me desire begins to consume my senses to fire up the motor and take a round-tripper through the country. That's when I say, "I have a *hankering* for a ride!" If the circumstances allow it, I usually respond. Afterward, I feel refreshed.

Though "hankering" may not sound sophisticated enough to grace the lips of the modern suburbanite, it is by no means extinct. If you traveled to my hometown, which sits along the Ohio River in West Virginia, you just might hear it. Your best opportunity would come if you happen to be near one of the locals who suddenly thinks of what is available at the local Dairy Queen.

They may say one of two things: "I have a hankering for a hot dog with sauce and slaw," or "Man, I have a serious hankering for a dip cone!"

For those who have been sadly deprived of one or both of these special culinary experiences, a description is in order. The hot dog comes on a steamed, white-bread bun. It is smothered with a ladleful of special chili sauce then topped with a generous helping of the sweetest coleslaw on the planet. It comes wrapped in heat-saving aluminum foil in either the foot-long size or the traditional length. Because the hot dogs are so well loved by countless souls who have enjoyed them through the years, they are often purchased, frozen, and transported to various parts of the nation to be shared with friends and family or, as I have been known to do, hoard them for later happiness.

The dip cone takes the sweet tooth craving to another level. First of all, it has to be consumed quickly. One rarely makes it off the Dairy Queen parking lot without most of it already put away. The reason is that the vanilla ice cream that is piled securely onto a crunchy, edible cone is carefully baptized in a pool of rich, dark, hot fudge. The outcome is a hard but fragile veneer of warm chocolate that immediately begins to melt the ice cream. Within seconds the white flow of joy starts running onto the hand that holds the cone. To successfully take in such delight requires plenty of fresh napkins and a lightning-fast tongue.

If my descriptions of these incredibly caloric treats have generated in you a desperate desire to pack your saddle-bags and head to West Virginia, then, my friend, you understand "hankering." I'm not sure what I would do if both urges came over me at the same time—to ride my bike and have a foot-long hot dog with sauce and slaw along with a dip cone for dessert. An 800-mile, round-trip trek from the Nashville area to the Mountaineer State would be a challenge, but I think I'd be willing to make the attempt!

Perhaps you have your own hankerings. While you and I may share at least one of them (motorcycles), the rest may be as unique to you as your thumbprint. This may be true, but there is one other desire I sincerely hope we have in common. It is found in 1 John 3:2-3:

> *Beloved, now we are children of God, and it has not appeared as yet what we will be. We know that when He appears, we will be like Him, because we will see Him just as He is. And everyone who has this hope fixed on Him purifies himself, just as He is pure.*

If you have a deep longing to see Christ when He appears, and you want to be ready when it happens, then we share a "holy hankering"! To see Jesus will be sweeter, by far, than rumbling on two wheels onto the parking lot of the Dairy Queen in my hometown.

Thank You, Father, for longings. May my greatest desire always be for the day when Your people are called into the presence of Your matchless Son. Make me ready to see Him. In His name I pray, amen.

> *The Son of Man is coming at an hour when you do not think He will.*
>
> Matthew 24:44

4

The Real Balloons

We are no longer to be children.

Ephesians 4:14

It would be impossible to count the number of valuable collectable baseball cards and my mother's clothespins I totally mangled in my younger years. As many as they may be, nothing else seemed to work as well in creating that special, artificial sound of a motorized cycle. With expert precision I would wrap a card around one of the down forks of my Schwinn bicycle so that part of the stiff paper extended into the spokes. Using a clothespin to secure it in place the clatter that was generated as the thin metal rods slapped across the color pictures of the baseball players created enough clatter to sufficiently disturb the neighbors. Adding more cards made it even louder. As I pedaled down the street I could be heard for half a block. The attention was glorious, and I thought I was big stuff. Then one day the boy with the balloons showed up!

I'll never forget sitting on our porch and hearing the low rumble coming up the street. I trembled in anticipation that a real live motorcycle was about to roll by. Was I ever surprised when Charlie, the kid from two streets behind me, went booming past on his Murray. With one balloon being pummeled by his rotating spokes he had taken the fantasy of motorcycling to the highest level a pedal pusher could carry it.

Inflated to just the right tightness and leaving enough excess on each end to tie around the down forks of his front frame, Charlie had found the secret to the CC impersonation. His bike had the rumble of at least a 650 motor. I was flabbergasted as I listened to him roar by. I went straightway and began rummaging through our house for some balloons.

Hark! There they were, buried in the drawer that held things like old greeting cards and birthday cake candles. Just two red beauties were all I found. Though I had not gotten a real good look at how Charlie had mounted his "engine" to his bike, it didn't take long for me to figure it out. I had to tie them on facing away from the hub then force them around and into the spokes as I turned the wheel.

Oh! How sweet the sound as I climbed on and headed down the pavement. For nearly two full blocks I was vice-king of the road…until…the rubber wall of the balloon got too thin to handle the sliding slap of the spokes. Pop! The rumble died. I needed more and better balloons.

Over time, Charlie and I became friends. We figured out that a little petroleum jelly on the balloons extended their lives. It was the noisiest summer on record in our part of town. It was also a season in my life that never ended. Finally, years later, something happened that was inevitable. What I had pretended to be at 12 years old, I now am. I'm still a "gear head," but of the motorcycle variety. Today, I have the real deal and the progression to it has been unforgettable. The journey has been from clothespins and baseball cards to party balloons to a light-weight scooter to a 550-pound, four-cylinder, five-speed, gasoline-burning beauty.

Some who might question my attraction to the world of two-wheeled wonders would contend that I have lived the first half of 1 Corinthians 13:11, "when I became a man," but I have ignored the second half of the verse which says, "I did away with childish things." However, those of us who push the start button on our grown-up versions of the cycle would be the first to retort, "This is serious business!" That sudden, explosive rumble under our seats eliminates any doubt that the machine beneath us is anything but pretend. The glorious sound is a wake-up call.

If the motorcycle has done nothing else for my brain, it has been an effective reminder that I can no longer "speak as a child, think as a child, or reason as a child." I cannot allow myself to take a juvenile approach to things. Allowing the gravity of this reality to find its way from the motor I straddle to the rest of my life is a wonderful benefit. My family, my job, my friendships, and, most important, my walk with Christ is serious business. I will admit that, though I am now a man, I smile like a little boy when my "Black Beauty" roars to life. I have a feeling you would, too!

Father in heaven, thank You for the gift of growing up. Thank You that I have been allowed to journey from the child years to the sobriety of being a man. Help me think, speak, and reason as an adult and be a responsible steward of these years.

We are to grow up in all aspects
into Him who is the head, even Christ.

Ephesians 4:15

5

At the Curb

*Without faith it is impossible
to please Him.*

Hebrews 11:6

One of the best pictures of living a life of faithful obedience to God can be found at the end of your driveway—especially if you own a motorcycle. How many times have you rolled the bike out of the garage for the sole purpose of a "joy" ride. As you near the street or highway in front of your house, you must come to grips with the fact that you have a choice to make. Do you go left or right? Although you may know the area well, if you're like me, you debate with yourself about which direction to head. At that moment, you are in a predicament that resembles that of Abraham as recorded in Hebrews 11:8: "By faith Abraham, when he was called, obeyed by going out to a place which he was to receive for an inheritance; and he went out, *not knowing where he was going*" (emphasis added).

It's hard to imagine how deeply Abraham had to trust the one who said "Go!" without letting him know exactly where he was supposed to end up. And I find it terribly tiring to think that his striking out involved a whole lot more than just putting on his sandals and coat and taking off. The passage says he dwelt in tents with a huge bunch of other travelers. That means he had some serious packing and unpacking to do as he obediently journeyed with God. It was not an easy task, and today we applaud Abraham's great faith.

Although my preparations are simple when I get ready for a ride (checking tire pressure, oil level, putting on gloves and a helmet), it's a great time to remember Abraham. As I sit at the curb, tweak the throttle, and decide my route, I am a reflection of his quest to follow the Lord. Although my delightful dilemma doesn't compare to the seriousness of Abraham's, it still reminds me that God wants me to be willing to trust Him to lead me in all areas of my life.

One time in particular that I recall following the lead of God in this way happened in late 1980. Prior to that year, I had been in a music group that traveled a lot. Annie and I had a child who was just entering toddlerhood. I knew I was absent far too much, and I was deeply troubled about being a "dad from a distance." I prayed earnestly about which way to turn. One day I sensed the call to leave the group and go home.

Although I was excited about knowing it was the right choice, I was scared out of my wits because I had no idea where to go in regard to my work. Still, I announced my resignation, "went to the curb," and waited on God's prompting. More than 20 years have gone by, and I can confidently say that I did the right thing. Two things give evidence that the choice was correct. One, by choosing to make them my priority, I didn't lose my relationship with our son and, eventually, with our daughter. Today, we are the best of friends. Second, the work I have been privileged to do with my wife in music has been pure joy. Had I not been willing to step out in faith all those years ago, I would have missed the joy of laboring by her side.

Perhaps you are feeling a call to ride somewhere. Maybe God is prompting you to fire up your motor and trust Him. Are you trembling in your spirit at the idea? If so, don't forget that by facing the challenge Abraham encountered in not knowing where he was going, you are in the company of a mighty patriarch. May God bless your faith as your engine idles at the curb.

Father in heaven, thank You for faith. With it I can trust You to lead me in the direction that is best for me and those who journey with me. Help me to trust You more. To Your glory I pray in Jesus' name, amen.

And He said to them, "Follow Me...."
Matthew 4:19

6

Wasn't It Smart of God to…?

I will give thanks to the LORD with all my heart;
I will tell of all Your wonders.

Psalm 9:1

When our children were living in our home, dinnertime was often more than just gobbling down the "beans and taters." It frequently turned into a sharing time that could range from serious to silly. Whichever took place, the conversations were always enjoyable and rewarding, often including a look at God's view of things (an intentional parental twist to the talks). Today's thoughts will cover one end of the spectrum, tomorrow's will swing to the other end. First, the not so serious.

As we neared the end of our meal one evening, we began the familiar sipping of drinks, picking at the crumbs on our plates, and verbally going over the events of the day. Not much had happened out of the ordinary so the conversation was a little bland. That was mom and dad's normal cue to take advantage of the moment and address something spiritual. I was fresh out of ideas and was pleasantly relieved when Annie chimed in with, "Let's play a game!" I was also a little surprised because she was more apt to talk about the weighty concerns our kids might be facing rather than heading to the lighter side. To me, "Let's play a game" sounded like some fun was about to happen. I was right.

Annie continued with her suggestion, and added, "The name of this game is 'Wasn't It Smart of God to...' and you finish the sentence." The kids smiled, sat up straight, and waited for more instructions.

"Let's take turns coming up with something God has done that is evidence of His incredible intelligence. I'll start. Wasn't it smart of God to...make our nose holes go down instead of up so when it rains we won't drown?"

Not only had Annie shocked us into some good laughter, she had delivered a nearly untopable first contribution to the list. However, the one thing she had overlooked was that she had two males at the table. Nathan and I took the idea of featuring body parts and ran with it like football half-backs. Our young teenage son offered, "Wasn't it smart of God to make the end of our index finger just smaller than our nose hole?"

It was my turn, but I had to gain my composure as I added, "Wasn't it smart of God to give us a tongue so when we talk we don't 'kown ike iz?'"

Heidi had already fallen into the "gross trap" that the two males had laid. "Wasn't it smart of God...to put our feet so far away from our noses?"

The rest of the evening went downhill from there in terms of discretion. Annie and I had to work hard at keeping things on a respectable level, although she had to make a greater effort than I. The following is a list of a few more of the things we came up with. Wasn't it smart of God to...

- give us armpits and gravity to keep our arms down?

- give men a receding hairline instead of an advancing one?

- make our lower jaw move when we talk instead of our upper jaw so we don't talk like this (a vigorous bobbing of the head while talking is required to complete this thought)?

• make our hair not bleed when we cut it?

• give us a bunch of pimples instead of one really big one (Nathan)?

• give us the teen years to make it easier for parents to let go of their children (Annie)?

• give us parents so the kids don't mind leaving home (Heidi)?

• give us a fever to tell us we're either sick or in love (Steve, facetiously looking at Annie)?

• make bears and snakes hibernate in the winter so that hunters can kill little defenseless animals in safety (Annie's attempt to steer away from body parts)?

• make us to sleep with our eyes closed so we won't see the person next to us sleeping with his mouth open (Steve's attempt to get back to body stuff)?

• make men bald over a long period of time instead of it happening all at once while you're out on a date (Nathan's contribution while looking at his dad)?

• give us shoulders to hold up our clothes (fashion-conscious Heidi)?

• sneeze out instead of in (Annie, falling into the "boys will be boys" trap)?

It was a most enjoyable game for all of us. And it was also an eye-opener to take a moment and think about how awesome a Creator we have. God really is smart!

Thank You, God, for the incredibly wise way You have made us. We are indeed fearfully and wonderfully made. And thank You for mealtimes. The food of fellowship sustains us. Blessed be Your holy name. In Jesus' name I pray, amen.

Oh, the depth of the riches
both of the wisdom and knowledge of God!

Romans 11:33

7

Will There Be Time?

*For You are my hope; O Lord GOD, You are
my confidence from my youth.*

Psalm 71:5

Another busy day was winding down as our family gathered together once again to enjoy supper. The conversation was jovial and the smiles were as plentiful as the potatoes that were flying out of the bowl and onto our plates. The kids were especially talkative, and their expressions of contentment to be with a couple of grownups gave warmth to their mom and dad's hearts. This was extra pleasing because both Nathan and Heidi were teenagers.

By the time we were ready for the sugar blast that comes with dessert, we were engaged in some very quality exchanges, the type that makes family time memorable. Feelings were on the upside, and the grins continued to paint the faces of our teens...until...somehow...the subject of the day's TV report about Israel and a Mideast crisis was mentioned.

Current events were often part of our table conversations. Whatever we heard about that was happening in the world seemed to get at least a brief amount of coverage by one of us. Our opinions about the topics were usually shared, and it was always interesting to hear what our young ones had to say about them.

On this particular evening, Annie began verbalizing her thoughts about the nation of Israel and her understanding of its place in the biblical scheme of the "end times." I joined in, and with wide-eyed excitement, Annie and I exhibited our thrill about the possibility that the "rapture" of the church of God could happen at any time. With that "snatching away" of believers, our lives here on the earth, as we knew them, would be replaced with our eternal existence with Christ. Heidi showed her keen interest in the hope as well by being inquisitive enough to ask questions. Nathan, on the other hand, suddenly got very quiet, sat back, and folded his arms. I was surprised.

I studied him out of the corner of my eye. I could tell that his demeanor was not at all that of a pouting teen. I had seen that unwelcome pose plenty of times—enough to identify it. Nathan's sudden change in mannerism revealed that he was sad. For the rest of the time at our table, he was uncommonly silent.

Later that evening, I went to Nathan and asked him about what had happened during dinner. I was curious to know his thoughts and was hopeful that his willingness to tell me might bring back the joy he had had before dessert was served. Because he didn't want to offend me by seeming uninterested in spiritual things, he hesitated at first. But then he forced himself to open his heart. What he shared with me was life-changing for an old codger who had lost sight of the feelings of a young man. The following lyric was written within hours of my conversation with my son. These words describe what he told me.

Will There Be Time?
I have a son, he heard me say,
"The Lord's return could be any day."

Then he thought for a while and told me the fear
That fills a young man's heart in his teenage years

Will there be time for dreams to come true
To follow the call the way that young men do
Will a girl love me the way Mama loves you
Will there be time for dreams to come true

Then I thought of the joys I've known down here
I can understand his fear
How can a young man with dreams ever be convinced
That heaven will be far better than all of this

Will there be time for dreams to come true
To follow the call the way that young men do
Will a child love me the way that I love you
Dad, will there be time for dreams to come true?[1]

While many of our mealtimes have yielded some perfectly appropriate silliness, the sobering food for thought I took in that evening has stayed with me ever since. To this day, I strive to remember that our young ones—not only our kids but yours as well—look to the future with bright eyes. They *want* to live on and know the joys of this life. In my older years, when my body is tired and becoming more broken by the year, smiling at the thought that the trumpet can sound at any minute is much easier to do. As we grownups embrace that glorious anticipation, may we not forget about those whose clocks have not ticked as many times as ours. Their dreams and hopes shouldn't be unnecessarily discouraged by our seasoned wish for heaven. In due time, they will understand why our eyes gaze skyward. Until then, may we be careful to let them dream.

Father in heaven, thank You for the presence of youth among us. As I take my steps that seem to be getting slower by the days, help me find joy in the dreaming eyes of youngsters. Help me not be a hindrance to their hopes; instead, make me a source for their guidance as they seek to follow You. In Jesus' name, amen.

O God, You have taught me from my youth;
and I still declare Your wondrous deeds.

Psalm 71:17

8

One More Hand

And indeed our fellowship is with the Father,
and with His Son Jesus Christ.

1 John 1:3

Though the huge 18-wheelers that pass me on the highway create enough wind turbulence to make me feel like my motorcycle is wiggling through Jell-O, in no way will I bad-mouth the big guys. One reason is because the cargo they're hauling could be anything from the ingredients that go into Annie's incredible biscuits to the special part my buddy ordered to get his bike back on the road. I very much appreciate the hard work the drivers are doing day after day, night after night.

One morning several years ago I got a glimpse of one of these big rig drivers as he rolled by me in Indiana. What I saw him doing in the cab puzzled me at first. It was Sunday, around nine o'clock, and the traffic was rather light as we approached each other. He had one hand partially raised as if he were asking a teacher if he could say something. His lips were moving as well. I'm sure he wasn't reaching for a CB microphone because he didn't raise his hand up any farther the entire two or three seconds I observed him.

I wondered what on earth he was doing...then it hit me. It was the day of the week when most folks who go to church are either already at the building or about ready to leave their homes and head that way.

My imagination ran wild as the mental snapshot of the driver stayed in my head for several miles. Although I can't be sure exactly what his raised hand meant, I made a guess. It ended up in the following lyric.

Sunday Morning Run

Well he's rollin' down the highway
On a Sunday morning run
He'll be back Monday
When this job is done
It's how he feeds his children
And the woman that he loves
Right now they are all he's thinking of

'Cause he wishes he could be there
He knows right where they are
At this very moment
They're singing from their hearts
Standing in the congregation
Where his family always goes
He'd be there if he could
But his family knows

There is one more voice
And it is raised
Above the roar of that diesel
Joining in the praise
And there is one more hand
Lifted to the Holy One
While the other hand is working at the wheel
On this Sunday morning run

He's got four hundred miles to go
Then he can turn it all around
But in the presence of the Lord he knows
He can still be very close
To the ones he loves
Standing in that crowd
And they have no doubt

There is one more voice
And it is raised
Above the roar of that diesel
Joining in the praise
And there is one more hand
Lifted to the Holy One
While the other hand is working at the wheel
On this Sunday morning run.[2]

As I thought of the driver who had unknowingly inspired me, I prayed for him. If I was right about the reason for his raised hand, one thing was true: The fellowship he was having with the Lord connected him in the Spirit of Christ not only to his family, but to me as well because I, too, am a believer in Jesus. What a joyous thought!

If a Sunday morning finds you in the wind-wash of a big rig, say a prayer for the one at the wheel. You never know, both of you might be in the presence of the Lord at the same moment.

Thank You, Lord, for those who traverse our highways in ser-
vice to us all. May You bless them, as well as the multitudes of
others who have to be at work on days when they'd much
rather be with family, especially on Your day. In Jesus' name,
keep them safe and draw them close to You. To Your glory,
amen.

But if we walk in the Light as He Himself is in the Light,
we have fellowship with one another, and the blood of
Jesus His Son cleanses us from all sin.

1 John 1:7

9

Sermon in the Stones

Trust in the LORD forever, for in GOD the LORD,
we have an everlasting Rock.

Isaiah 26:4

One of my favorite places on the planet to explore from the saddle of my bike is right here in middle Tennessee. Highways 48, 49, and 13 are just a few of the ribbons of pavement that offer some of the nicest mixtures of twisties and straight-stretches available to the cycling world.

On occasion, when the road is unbending for a half- or three-quarters of a mile and doesn't require my utmost attention, I enjoy taking a moment to check out the scenes on the other side of the fences that line the routes. In all the miles on our back roads I have logged, I've noticed one particular sight that is repeated over and over again. Standing alone in abandoned lots, towering high above the uncut grasses that usually hug their bases, are the remains of what used to be houses. Everything else around those once-formed structures is gone, rotted away with the years. All that is left are the chimneys.

It would be hard to number how many of these lonely old smokestacks I have seen through the years. Although they vary in color and height, their shape is usually the same. They are broad at the bottom and slightly tapered at the top. Their longevity testifies to the ingenuity that went into their construction. Without a doubt, the people who designed them are to be commended for such quality engineering.

Besides ridding a house of unwanted, dark and dusty fumes, there were other important functions a chimney performed. Very often the warmth that was generated was the only source of comfort on cold winter days and was considered a valuable luxury to those who once gathered around it. Cooking over the heat that the flames provided, reading by the light that frolicked in the pit, and even some storytelling that took place around the dancing glow of the blaze made the hearth the center point of a home. Undoubtedly it was considered a true friend to all who dwelled inside the walls.

While I acknowledge how much fireplaces warmed the souls of those gathered, what strikes me most about the chimneys is how they have so significantly outlived the rugged timbers that made up the homes. Hard oak and poplar, as quality of wood as they are, cannot compete with the material in chimneys.

The key to the survival of the hearths, of course, is in the rock. Only the resiliency of stone could withstand the devastating effects of the years of wind and weather that pounded from without. Only rock could have survived the relentless, red-hot flames that tried from within to melt their form. In the face of all types of adversity, the carefully placed pile of rocks stubbornly refused to fall. Such is the enduring power of our God.

Like a preacher in a pulpit, the old, stony towers that grace our Tennessee fields are crying out like a sermon, saying, "Though time will consume your house and even the occupants within it, don't forget that God alone will be left standing when all else is gone. For that reason, make Him the most important part of your home. You can gather around Him when the fierce cold of uncertainty invades. There's light in Him in the darkness of life. You'll find food for your spirit at His hearth. And the warming fires of compassion for one another can be found in His bosom. God alone is the everlasting rock."

The next time you're cruisin' down the open highway and catch a glimpse of one of these monuments to endurance, let the sight remind you of the qualities of the "Rock of Ages."

Oh God, my mighty, everlasting Father, thank You that Your love for me has endured the harshness of time. You stand alone as the only wise, true, and faithful God. May my life testify of Your goodness today. In Your Son's name, amen.

> Is there any God besides Me,
> or is there any other Rock? I know of none.
>
> Isaiah 44:8

10

He Reigns

*And it happened after a while that the brook dried up,
because there was no rain in the land.*

1 Kings 17:7

Then I shall give you rains in their season...

Leviticus 26:4

The LORD reigns...

Psalm 93:1

I called my parents' house a few years ago during a hot summer month. I'll never forget the exchange that took place when my mother answered.

"How's the weather up in West Virginia today, Mom?"

"Pretty dry up here, Son."

I could tell I was being set up to ask, "How dry is it?"

"Oh! It's so dry that the Baptists are sprinklin' and the Methodists are using a damp cloth!"

We both got a good chuckle out of her well-delivered punch line. That summer was a hot one for everybody in our region. My poor, cracked-and-hardened yard was showing the effects of weeks without a drop of moisture. Even the mornings that usually left the ground with at least a thin blanket of dew were bone dry.

I can recall how the farmers were suffering...and praying. Their requests for showers were steady and heartfelt. My wife, Annie, was especially sympathetic to their plight because she grew up on a dairy farm and one of her family's means of feeding the cattle was accomplished by planting and harvesting corn. She says, "I can't remember a time that we weren't either praying for rain or begging God to make it stop. It seemed it was never just right—but the dry times were extra tough."

When I take a summer day's ride on my bike through the sweltering farmlands of our state and the soil is obviously thirsty, I share Annie's empathy for those who toil the ground. Last year I motored out to a friend's farm where I often go to hunt and, as he wiped the salty, August sweat off his forehead, he remarked about the damage that the absence of rain had made on his crops. When I got home and alerted Annie that we needed to join them in prayer, she responded with a sentence that began with, "I hope the Lord will touch their hearts and remind them that..." The words that came next were so profound I knew they would be a great encouragement to our friends. I went straight to my desk and used them as the title for the following song.

Even When It Does Not Rain, He Reigns

It's dry as bone this year in the fields
And the wind, it seems to be winning
Like a thief without mercy, it's come to steal
And blow away our living

But Babe, you and me, we've been here before
We are no strangers to the dust
It's time we take these thirsty fields to the Lord
Who else can we trust?

'Cause even when it does not rain, He reigns
Even when it does not rain, God reigns
He's the Master of the wind, He knows our names
And even when it does not rain, He reigns

Well, Darlin', I suppose there's not been a year
That we haven't prayed these fields through the weather
I wish there was a way we could use this flood of tears
That you and I have cried together

But, Babe, you and me, we've been here before
We are not strangers to this dust
But sometimes it's in the darkest hours
That we've clearly seen the Lord
And we know He's able to deliver us

'Cause even when it does not rain, He reigns
Even when it does not rain, God reigns
He's the Master of the wind, He knows our names
Even when it does not rain, He reigns![3]

The good news is that even with the less than perfect
weather, our friend's crop of soybeans found good favor
when he delivered them to the grain mill in late Sep-
tember. He saw it as a miracle, and we were glad we
joined him in trusting God with the yield.

But the lack of rain doesn't just affect workers of the
land. Regardless of the type of "farm" where a person
labors, it's important to understand that droughts can also
be financial, emotional, and relational. They come to all
folks. If it rains on the just, as well as the unjust, then it is
safe to say that dry spells will also fall on all of us at some
time. (See Matthew 5:45.) No matter what our circum-
stances are, our dependency ultimately must be on the
one who gave us the fields to plow. When we trust Him,
we can indeed take comfort in knowing that He reigns—
even when it doesn't rain!

Father in heaven, blessed be Your name for all Your provisions for us. Thank You for the days when the rain pours its refreshment into the soil of our lives. And thank You for those days that are so dry that we are made to look heavenward for relief. Help us keep our eyes fixed on You. In Jesus' name, amen.

Say among the nations, "The Lord reigns."

Psalm 96:10

11

Eternally Correct

Every word of God is tested; He is a shield to those who take refuge in Him. Do not add to His words....

Proverbs 30:5-6

Motorcycle terminology hasn't changed much through the years. Words like "chopper," "ape hanger," "bobbers," "foot paddling," and "solid-mounted" have survived many decades. And not much change can be expected as time rolls on. While this kind of consistency in word usage can be found in the world of cycling, it has not happened in the rest of society.

To illustrate, in the past I would buy a *used car*. Now I am in the market for a *pre-owned vehicle*. When I was a kid I went to a place called a *barber shop* for a *haircut*. Today I go to places like "The Mane Attraction" or "Hair Dynamics" for a *styling*. And *footwear* used to be shoes, *window dressings* were just curtains, and *eating establishment*s were local diners.

To be honest, I get weary of trying to keep up with the changes. Besides, some of them are downright ridiculous. There's a stubborn streak in me that refuses to say, "Let's do lunch," when, for years, I have said, "Let's go get a bite."

Perhaps one reason I am so tired with the way society is trying to alter my language is because so many of the new replacement terms are nothing more than attempts to cover the element of embarrassment over a matter. I am not, for example, ashamed that I am balding. That's right, I said it! My head is getting slicker than snot on a doorknob. I am not, as some would prefer to say, "follicly challenged." What's the big deal? I absolutely refuse to feel like less of a man when I see the ads that talk about a fellow's need for a "hair replacement system." That's a process I used to call "getting a rug." No offense to those who have done it, but let me feel virile in spite of my lack of locks.

Then there's this one: "He's gone postal." It's the new way of saying, "The man is out of control." Too bad for all the fine, upstanding, Post Office employees who get such a bad rap. I resent it for them. Why can't we say, "He's gone Ford assembly line!" I'm sure a few of those folks have been known to bean a buddy or two with a flying wrench.

Another allegedly new and improved phrase that annoys me is, "I've got issues." As far as I'm concerned, this one drags the bottom of the lake. I remember the day when, without feeling totally belittled, I could admit, "I have a problem!" What's so bad about openly disclosing the need for help? For those who are no longer brave enough to tell it like it is, I say, "Here's a tissue for your issue!"

I will concede that when it comes to some of the new verbiage, it is perfectly fine to "eat the Popsicle and leave the stick." *Mentally challenged*, for example, does sound more compassionate. While phrase replacements like these can be justified, I contend that for the most part it's time to stop beating around the verbal bush. I am afraid that our society's insatiable desire to sound "politically correct" (a new term that often means "I don't have much of a backbone") is leading to a dangerously weak way of dealing with God's spoken mandates.

For example, instead of using the well established "for all have sinned and fall short of the glory of God…" (Romans 3:23), one overly modern minister tried to make transgressors feel less threatened with "for everyone has misguided intentions and has not reached their full cosmic potential." Come on, give me a power nap! This type of ear tickling is not going to cut it. I just can't imagine God altering His words to mollycoddle the truth. For instance, "You would do well to consider your inner condition" will never be as strong and compelling as, "You must be born again!" (John 3:7).

"If God said it, it's good enough for me" is a familiar adage that can strengthen the spiritual spine of anyone who has been weakened in his or her willingness to tell it like it is. For the sake of the integrity of God's written truth that can set us free, all of us would do well to leave His words just the way we found them. Can I hear an "amen"? If I must choose whether to be politically or eternally correct, I'll take the latter.

Lord, thank You for Your kind forgiveness for those times I have tried to soft sell the hard facts about You. Help me be wise when I speak about You and Your ways. When I need to be gentle, lead me to Your gentle words. When I need to be bold, guide me to Your strong words. In Jesus' name I pray, amen.

> *Heaven and earth will pass away,*
> *but My words will not pass away.*
> Matthew 24:35

12

Inadvertent Watermelons

For whatever a man sows, this he will also reap.

Galatians 6:7

I'm always looking for a good excuse to fire up my Magna 750 and grace our local highway with its smooth presence. Just a trip to the grocery store gets me excited. It was during one of my treks to the Piggly Wiggly two summers ago that I made a tasty discovery. Even though my universal bag restricted me to a few items such as bread, milk, and cereal, I found that with enough bungie cords and a good sense of balance I could add a watermelon to the shopping list. As a result, the combination of my thirst for a ride and my hunger for watermelon resulted in our family consuming more than its fair share of the red-ripe delight.

What to do with so many leftover, hollowed out hulls became a dilemma. Fortunately, the open, unmowed field next to our house was a perfect dumping ground. It would be hard to number how many melon scraps were tossed there through the season.

When the next summer came around, we decided to start mowing the field. As I slowly cut through the heavy grass, I noticed an unusual growth. The long arms of the unfamiliar weeds reached out from a center point and the leaf was rather large. My curiosity was piqued, so I turned off the riding mower engine and inspected the unusual weed.

Much to my amazement, it wasn't a weed at all. It was watermelon vines! At least, that's what my farmer's daughter wife Annie told me when she came to help identify the growth. Without really trying, we had ourselves a melon farm within 50 yards of our back door!

Upon closer examination of the plants, I found several little baby green balls attached to the vines under the protective shadows of the broad leaves. My heart melted at their sight. They were so cute! I felt like I was a father-to-be—well, almost. Whenever I mowed, I put the rider in the slowest gear possible as I carefully skirted the nest of tasty toddlers.

The close-cut two acres of grass was always quite a contrast to the five or so clumps of sprawling vegetation that rose about a foot above the ground. Though our yard looked a little strange from the highway, I wasn't about to harm my darling little ones.

I cannot explain how exciting it was to harvest that first melon from our personal patch. With a bit of ceremony we sliced through the basketball-sized yield and held our breath in anticipation of its color, texture, and taste. We were not disappointed. It was a ripe, red-letter day for us to have eaten something so sweet from our own ground. In that moment, I connected with all others who have known the joy of farming!

I called our little crop our "inadvertent watermelons." I had no idea I had sown the seed, yet something good and nourishing came of it. What a great picture of those times in our lives when, without realizing it, a good seed has been planted and it yielded a worthwhile crop.

One of the best examples of this positive side of the "whatsoever you sow, you will reap" passage is found in a story told in a country song. It begins with the account of an older lady whose car was broken down on the highway. A young man comes along and helps her get it back into running condition. She offers him money for his help, and he politely refuses.

Farther down the road the woman stops at a small cafe to get something to eat, and she sees that the waitress who is serving her is obviously pregnant and very tired. When she finishes with her meal and is about to leave a tip, she remembers the young man's generous assistance. To honor him she leaves an uncommonly large tip and passes along his heart of kindness.

The ballad ends with the mother-to-be telling her husband about the elderly lady and her bountiful tip. As it turns out, the young man in the story was the young woman's husband. His seed of kindness on the highway had unexpectedly borne good fruit.

Father in heaven, thank You for those times in my life when the deeds I didn't see as extraordinary yielded an unexpected blessing, a sweet reward. You alone deserve the credit. Bless You! In Jesus' name, I pray, amen.

He who sows sparingly will also reap sparingly; and he who sows bountifully will also reap bountifully.

2 Corinthians 9:6

13

Stately Pair

Even so, every good tree bears good fruit.
Matthew 7:17 NKJV

If you are ever on your bike and traveling into or out of Nashville, Tennessee, on Interstate 24, on the west side of the city, you'll pass Exit 19. If time allows you to peel off the 4-lane and point your front tire to the southeast, I suggest you ride about seven miles down the road. It is there, on your right, about a half mile before the T in the road that you'll see my parents.

Actually, they are not there in bodily form but a very good representation of them can be seen. Standing side by side, tall and strong, in a large field are two of the prettiest oak trees in all of Tennessee. Each time I motor past that spot and take in the sight of the pair, I think of some characteristics they possess that closely resemble those of my father and mother.

First of all, like the very mature trees, my folks have stood together more than 53 years. Faithful to one another's presence, they have never wandered away. Individually and mutually they have fought against the attacks of heavy winds, devastating droughts, sicknesses, and the ravaging effects of time in order to maintain their status as a couple.

How could the oaks have stood so long together? The answer is found in their roots that run deep into the soil.

As if they know their source of strength comes from heaven, they lift their arms day and night, without fail, in praise of the Giver of Life. The same is true for my parents. They know their lives are sustained by God's amazing grace. Not only are the arms of their hearts always directed to God in praise, very often they literally lift their hands in thanksgiving to Him—and Him alone!

The second way my folks are like those oaks is in the way the trees have provided shelter for other living things that have come to them through the years. Their leaves and branches have been a resting place. Their shade has been a relief from the heat. Their lives have yielded much food for the hungry ones who have depended upon their yield. This, too, is a picture of my mother and father. How grateful I am that I was one of the privileged few to know the care they've given to others throughout their lives. It has blessed me physically and spiritually.

As a gift to my parents on the occasion of their fifty-second anniversary, I motored out to the site and took a picture of the two oaks. After getting it developed, I mounted it to my easel and, using it as a reference, went to work on an acrylic paint interpretation of the scene. I call the finished product "The Stately Pair."

Using lots of green color, I depicted the steadfast trees in the summer season, full of foliage, when life is at its peak. I wanted the painting to represent the time I lived in my folks' protective arms.

Now things are different. My folks have moved on through summertime, but they certainly haven't lost their beauty. In fact, I would have to say that just as it is true that the two mighty oaks on Highway 256 are their finest when their leaves have taken on the blaze of autumn, my parents are at their best today. All the brilliant hues of experience now grace their lives. The yellows of caution, the reds of passion, the greens of sweet memories of earlier years, and the browns of their awareness that life has its limits are the colors I see when I look at them. Such beauty, such dignity.

I want my marriage to Annie to be like those two oaks and the couple they represent to me. If we can accomplish such a goal, I know our standing together will be a picture of hope to our children. In order for us to accomplish this, though, our roots must run deep into God's ground. What an honor it would be to have others look at us and say, "There grows a 'stately pair.'"

What a blessing You have given to those of us whose parents have been so faithful to grow together in Your field. I pray earnestly for all who do not know this kind of joy. May their hearts find the delight of knowing Your great provision and protection.

Thank You for the shelter I found in the lives of my folks. Help me to be faithful to the one You planted me beside so that we can grow together as testament to Your mighty power. In Jesus' name, amen.

Honor your father and mother.
Exodus 20:12

14

The Verb

*I in them and You in Me, that they may be perfected in
unity, so that the world may know that You sent Me, and
loved them, even as You have loved Me.*

John 17:23

I've heard it said that the word "believer" is a not a noun;
it is a verb. When a person yields his life to Christ, he is
not immediately turned into a stationary thing, like a
statue, and put on display. Much to the contrary, a
believer in Christ becomes an active, mobile container of
the Spirit of our living Savior.

A clear picture of this is found in the person who
becomes a motorcyclist. The individual is not suddenly
bronzed and placed like a mannequin on the seat of a
decommissioned cycle and placed as a piece of art in a
museum. Not at all! The new representative of the
cycling family engages in major movement.

As proof that the biker has become a verb, consider
what he or she must do to get the machine in motion.
The left hand is busy with the clutch, the left foot is
clicking through the gears, the right hand is rotating the
throttle or squeezing the brake lever, and the right foot
adds to the mix its braking ability. All the gyrations necessary to get the wheels rolling or to get them stopped
would make any nonrider feel dizzy and intimidated at
the thought of how "verbish" one must be to wear the
name of "cyclist." A biker is many parts acting as one.

As believers in the living Lord, there is also much to be doing. And, similar to the biker, the entire body is involved. The ears hear the call, the feet follow, the hands help others, the knees know when to hit the floor in prayer, the tongue talks of His saving grace, and the mind makes decisions moment by moment regarding righteous living.

To carry this picture to the next logical level, "church" should also be a verb. When the church is at its best, it is not a steepled, multimillion dollar monument made of steel, bricks, and mortar equipped with escalators, elevators, and state-of-the-art technology. Rather, the church is at its truest form when all its members are doing their prescribed jobs.

When the teachers are teaching, when the preachers are preaching, the cleaners are cleaning, the deacons are "deaking," and the singers are singing—then the church is moving and fulfilling its purpose. Each member must cooperate. Just as a biker's left hand should not announce to his left foot, "I'm going to go home now," none of the church's "body parts" can cease their duties and expect the machine to keep going. And, when the unified functioning of the church spills outside the walls of its meeting place and each of its members are touching the lives of the lost, then the church is making the ultimate impact on the world.

The next time you clutch, throttle, shift gears, and brake, remember the picture you are being of both the believer and the body of Christ!

Thank You, Father, for the need we have for a unified body, rightly working together and moving through time with Your

purpose as our chief goal. Help us depend on Your strength and guidance to accomplish the tasks You set before us. Bless us with Your grace to keep the machine of ministry in motion. In Christ's name, amen.

That they may be one, just as We are one.

John 17:22

15

The Bultaco Blessing

You were faithful with a few things, I will put you in charge of many things; enter into the joy of your master.

Matthew 25:21

Today's verse contains a principle that can be beneficial to *every* area of our lives. If I had followed the wisdom in the verse, I would have chosen a 75cc Yamaha dirt bike instead of the huge Bultaco in my friend's garage for my first motorcycle ride. The fellow whose chain link fence and corner yard were damaged by my inexperience would agree. And my wallet wouldn't have been squashed even flatter by the cost of the repairs. This "Bultaco Blessing" would be reiterated in my career and my spiritual life.

Starting with the smaller things and growing to the big things is an undeniable bit of biblical wisdom that can be taken from today's verse—and all of us would do well to follow it. This will help us avoid all sorts of pain and heartache. But that's not the only incredible truth that can be gleaned from Matthew 25:21. A wonderful insight is available for the person who, after years of faithfully performing a certain task day after day, might be wondering, *When do I get to enjoy the "big things" part of the principle?* Maybe it's already happened! Let me illustrate.

As a group of young, aspiring musicians in the mid-seventies, my three friends and I would sit in a booth at the Nashville Music Row area I-Hop Pancake House and state and restate our music business goals to one another. As we slowly ate our cheap meal of flapjacks and coffee, the tone of the conversation would usually vacillate between hopeful and helpless. We were destitute when it came to necessities such as industry contacts, equipment, transportation, proper stage apparel, and influence. Furthermore, the money it took to buy all that stuff was missing, too. Though we were poor in our pockets, our hearts were rich with dreams. One of the things that kept us pressing on in spite of our lack of resources was our belief that God would hold up His end of the "small things to big things" bargain.

Days turned to weeks, weeks to months, and months to years without the kind of success we thought we were supposed to have received by being faithful. Still, we journeyed the highways of America fulfilling our call, singing before groups that were not impressive in numbers—but the size of the hunger in their hearts for the encouragement we could offer was huge. So we kept on "pickin' and grinnin'" for nearly five years.

I'd like to say that the band eventually got its big break. Instead, it broke up in late 1980. We sensed that the Lord was finished with us as a group, and we each agreed to quietly go our separate ways. I was the only one who stayed on the music road.

Though I have intentionally not dwelt too long on the thought, I have to be honest and confess that I wondered why God didn't allow us the level of success others have known. I silently carried that question in my heart for quite a while before it faded away. By then, my wife and I were in full swing with our musical ministry and, just like the earlier group I was in, the venues where we sang were not cavernous concert halls. Instead, most of them were intimate church sanctuaries.

Then one day, about three or four years ago, that haunting question returned: "Whatever happened to the 'big things' that faithfulness is supposed to yield?" I went back to the passage and reread it. That's when it hit me like a ton of guitars. God had indeed kept His end of the deal. How did I come to this realization? I had been misquoting the verse to myself all these years. I finally noticed that it says "few things/many things" not "small things/big things!" I suddenly realized that the passage requires a *collective* look at faithfulness, not just a view of a single era of a person's life. When I looked back through the years and recalled the huge number of small concerts in obscure places I had played with my former band and with Annie, I began to understand that God had turned a host of "few things" into an accumulation of many things. My heart filled with joy at the thought of how God had been faithful to His promise.

Today I see "success" through different eyes. Delivering the truth of God's Word in the form of a song or story before a small audience is a cherished opportunity. Why? Because being faithful to that setting gives me one more of the "few things" to add to the divine collection. Based on that premise, I encourage everyone from pastors to entrepreneurs, from teachers to musicians who feel less than successful, to take a fresh look at how God has worded this concept.

Father, thank You for showing me the truth in Your Word. The comfort of knowing that You always keep Your promises is

a blessing to my weary spirit. Forgive me for ever doubting You. Help me remain faithful to the few things so that someday I can hear You say, "Enter into the joy of your master." In Jesus' name, amen.

> Blessed is that servant whom his master,
> when he comes, will find so doing.

Matthew 24:46 NKJV

16

Near Miss

This man might have been set free.
Acts 26:32

Most of us who travel the busy skies of our nation know very well that a "near miss" doesn't refer to a man landing a seat assignment next to an attractive lady. Instead, the words make each of us quietly tremble inside at the thought that somewhere above us two heavy planes almost collided. The result would have been a fiery rain of metal and flesh. Just to imagine it sends a chill up my spine.

Not too long ago I discovered that a near miss is not limited to the clouds. It can happen right down here on the ground. I was tooling down a country road that has an enjoyable number of nice hills and curves. Just as the banks of the highway that had risen on each side began to flatten out, I got a glimpse of movement out of the corner of my full-face helmet. I didn't think too much of it until it was almost too late. Suddenly a deer was airborne and, as is often the case during a potential disaster, everything seemed to slow down.

Although I love to hunt deer, I don't prefer to do it with a "Honda 06"! I'll not forget the sight of the doe as she sailed over my front tire. My 45-mile-per-hour speed quickly closed the distance between my windshield and

61

her sleek body. As she seemed to hang in midair like a wrecking ball in front of me, I took in a deep breath and wondered what to do. Out of a natural reaction, I instantly squeezed and stepped on the brakes and ducked my head as her sharp, hind feet nearly brushed across my plastic-covered face. I almost had to pull off the road to settle down and keep from hyperventilating. That close call tampered with my nerves for the rest of the day.

Whether a near miss takes place in the unfriendly skies or on a critter-crowded highway, everyone is happy that it didn't happen. However, there is another type of collision that, if it doesn't happen, the outcome is eternal tragedy—a disaster of major proportions. It is an impact every person should wish for:

> "King Agrippa, do you believe in prophets? I know that you do believe." Then Agrippa said to Paul, "You almost persuade me to become a Christian." And Paul said, "I would to God that not only you, but also all who hear me today, might become both almost and altogether such as I am, except for these chains" (Acts 26:27-29 NKJV).

King Agrippa had a near miss with the joy of knowing the everlasting salvation that comes through giving all to Christ. How much better off the king would have been had his will collided with God's grace. Unfortunately, the encounter cost the king his place in heaven, the worst tragedy any person can experience.

Perhaps you have had some close calls in your life, either on the road or somewhere else. As you look back on them and feel a deep sense of gratitude for having skirted physical disaster, it is my hope that the day your heart was on a collision course with God's convicting power concerning your sin, you did have a head-on meeting with His forgiveness! Its divine impact results in eternal joy!

Father, thank You for the day my stubborn will ran headlong into Your lovingkindness. The result has been the greatest joy I have ever known. To be assured that I am Yours and I will meet You when all is said and done is a blessing beyond measure. May my life reflect the delight of meeting You. In Jesus' name, amen.

For the Son of Man has come to seek
and to save that which was lost.

Luke 19:10

17

The Fearful Rider

The fear of the LORD prolongs life.
Proverbs 10:27

Someone once asked me, "Do you really enjoy riding a motorcycle?" The way they posed the question seemed to indicate they may have considered trying it at one time but couldn't muster the nerve to make the attempt. All their apprehensions, if they had any, were probably confirmed when I answered, "I thoroughly enjoy my motorcycle, but I am never totally relaxed on it." It was the most honest response I could give.

Essentially, I ride in fear. It's not the kind of fear that keeps me away from my bike. It's the type that makes me keenly aware that I must never forget what's under me. No matter how sunny the day, how perfect the temperature, or how deserted the highway is, there is always a good reserve of respect in me for the iron animal I straddle. Knowing that the combined weight of my body and bike is nearly 800 pounds, and that a task like stopping it in the event of an emergency is serious business, it would be far too dangerous to be overly casual with the ride. For that reason, my eyes scan the area ahead of me like radar, and I constantly check the rearview mirrors to monitor the goings on behind me.

Another little thing I habitually do in order to be safer is to watch the hubcap of any car that appears to be waiting to enter the highway from a side road. If their wheel makes even the slightest movement, I'm on the brakes. In addition, I also slow down a little as I approach the situation.

This necessary "fear" of the motorcycle doesn't start when I let the clutch out and roll the throttle. It begins when I first decide to go somewhere, then it escalates when I open the garage door and enter its holding area. All I have to do is walk toward my bike with the intentions of firing up the motor and my heart rate rises. It is with a certain amount of ceremonial trepidation that I turn the ignition key then push the start button. I realize this sounds a little eccentric, but the respect for the bike has so saturated my thinking that I cannot go about it any other way.

Although it may be extremely important for a biker to cultivate a high level of respect for a cycle, there are at least two spiritual benefits to be gained by it. The first is that a rider's innate and immense regard for his machine makes him a prime candidate for having a clearer understanding of the human need to maintain a healthy fear of God. Any rider who embraces fear as the first step toward properly handling a bike is ahead of others who have no concept of the need for reverence. This same rider need only take a small step to find the glorious truth of Proverbs 9:10: "The fear of the LORD is the beginning of wisdom."

The second advantage cyclists have when it comes to fearing God is that they personally know their very lives depend on maintaining a high level of precaution. A fearful cyclist will probably last longer than a fearless one, for obvious reasons. By embracing this attitude, a biker doesn't have to go a long way to agree that "the fear of the

LORD prolongs life." In the way that being a fearful rider makes a person act responsibly when the wheels are rolling, being a fearful pilgrim will greatly influence the way one walks with God.

Although being a conscientious biker can contribute to becoming a more committed believer, the flip side of this thought might interest someone who has yet to give a motorcycle a try. Anyone who lives with an undying reverence for God would make a prime candidate for becoming a biker. Why? Because he understands the need for and the benefits of fear. Ladies and gentlemen, start your engines!

Oh, God, You alone are the one and only true and all-powerful God. I bow before You today and admit that there is no other god before You (including my motorcycle). Please protect me as I ride and when I enter into Your holy presence. I know that I can come to You only because I am clothed with the blood-bought righteousness of Your Son, Jesus. May my years be prolonged because I fear You. In Christ's name I pray, amen.

The fear of the LORD leads to life,
so that one may sleep satisfied, untouched by evil.

Proverbs 19:23

18

Watch Where You Aim

*How long will you love what is worthless
and aim at deception?*

Psalm 4:2

Before I got my first full-size bike, I was talking to a gentleman who had recently purchased a Gold Wing. In his early 60s, he had finally yielded to a lifelong desire to feel the open highway on two wheels. As we stood and jawed about riding skills and such, he told me, "I must warn you about one of the first hard lessons I encountered. I was traveling on a road just past the outskirts of town when I saw a billboard straight ahead of me that had some information about an event I wanted to attend. As I was taking the opportunity to memorize the dates, without knowing it, I had come to a 90-degree corner doing about 45 miles per hour. Needless to say, I left the road and plowed through a fence right under the big sign. The harm done to my bike was some considerable fairing damage, and I had a few scratches. But the worst hurt was my severely wounded ego. Thankfully, that was the extent of it."

I was all-ears as he related this incident to me. He could tell he had my full attention, and added, "Steve, whatever you do, remember you will usually go where you're looking when on a bike! Be careful where you aim it."

His advice was well taken and to this day, every time I find my eyes focusing too long on a sight that is outside the lines of the road, I see that gentleman's face in my memory. I consider my meeting him, hearing his words of warning, and seeing his facial expression as he passionately said them as one of the most important moments in my motorcycle history. This same advice is found in the question asked in Psalm 4:2. As you reread it, I urge you to receive it as a fair warning about the dangers of setting your sights on sin. To do so is to eventually head in that direction. Consider James' warning: "But each one is tempted when he is carried away and enticed by his own lust. Then when lust has conceived, it gives birth to sin; and when sin is accomplished, it brings forth death" (James 1:14-15). The progression described here is a deadly one.

How can we avoid the spiritual injuries that result from gazing at sin? The first thing a follower of Christ must do is stay alert. The fellow who rode his Gold Wing under the billboard tells us not to be mesmerized by the "stuff" off the highway, no matter how interesting it is. Scripture does the same in 1 Peter 5:8: "Be of sober spirit, be on the alert. Your adversary, the devil, prowls around like a roaring lion, seeking someone to devour." Keeping our eyes fixed on Jesus, "the Narrow Way," is our dependable safeguard. When we're looking at Him, we are not going to wander off the road to pleasing God.

There are as many unwholesome things that can capture a believer's attention as there are believers to be enticed by them. That being true, an important question to ask is, "What is the sin that so easily draws me aside?" As we ask ourselves this, may we commit together to get our eyes back on the highway of holiness so that when the "temptation corners" come we can lean in on God's strength and make our way safely around them. If we don't watch where we aim our hearts, we'll be picking dirt and splinters out of our souls!

Father in heaven, I want to be one of Your alert ones. Thank You for Your Holy Spirit who pricks my heart with a moment-by-moment reminder that I am a follower of the righteous one. Please keep encouraging me to act like it by being a watchman over my soul and my mind. In Jesus' wonderful name, amen.

Lay aside every encumbrance and the sin which so easily entangles us, and let us run with endurance the race that is set before us.

Hebrews 12:1

19

Heart Markers

*Then Joshua set up twelve stones in the middle of the
Jordan…and they are there to this day.*

Joshua 4:9

I'm not quite sure what it is about the way I'm wired that
makes me do it, but I enjoy leaving signs of my having
passed by a place. I do it only if it has some special
meaning to me. For example, there are little heaps of
small stones along the Appalachian Trail where I've
walked with my children. On another occasion I put four
quarters in a baggie and buried them at the end of a
bridge along a highway far from home where we bicycled
on a multiday trip. These are marks that testify to the fact
that we have been there together and survived the journey.
Today, when I motorcycle the secondary roads of Tennessee, one thing I like to do is stop and check my
highway marks. I inspect their condition and enjoy
recalling why the place holds such importance. Actually,
my somewhat quirky behavior has a scriptural prece-
dence! Today's verse, for example, is a reference to
Joshua's placing of the 12 stones at the Jordan River
where God parted the waters so the ark could cross safely
over. God instructed Joshua to create a marker for a good
reason, which is found in Joshua 4:6-7. "Let this be a sign
among you, so that when your children ask later, saying,
'What do these stones mean to you?' then you shall say to
them, 'Because the waters of the Jordan were cut off…'

so these stones shall become a memorial to the sons of Israel forever." The stones testify of God's deliverance, reminding those who saw them or heard about them that they, too, must depend on Him.

In 1 Samuel 7, the account is given of how God "thundered with a great thunder on that day against the Philistines and confused them, so that they were routed before Israel. The men of Israel went out of Mizpah and pursued the Philistines, and struck them down..." (verses 10-11). That's when Samuel left a mark on the territory. Verse 12 explains: "Then Samuel took a stone and set it between Mizpah and Shen, and named it Ebenezer, saying, 'Thus far the LORD has helped us.'"

In another passage, found in the book of Genesis, it is reported that Jacob "set up a pillar in the place where [God] had spoken with him, a pillar of stone, and he poured out a drink offering on it; he also poured oil on it. So Jacob named the place where God had spoken with him, Bethel" (Genesis 35:14-15).

While there are a few special spots on the planet I could physically take you to and tell you why they mean so much to me, there are many more Ebenezers and Bethels in my heart that I would rather show you. Unfortunately it doesn't require a long motorcycle ride to get to them, but I can take you to places in time where God showed Himself faithful to deliver me. And I'm not the only one who has these heart markers that show God's gracious deliverance.

I recently met Oakley and Lois Korbelik in Kerrville, Texas. They told me of an incident that occurred after a Christian Motorcycle Association (CMA) meeting when they lived in Kansas. The monthly gathering was an hour's ride from their home, so they normally didn't stay for the traditional after-meeting ice cream run. However, one evening they both felt, for some unknown reason, that they should remain and join the group. As motorcyclists often do, they got caught up in the joy of more fellowship and conversation and ran out of time to go for the sweet treat. After about 30 minutes they both felt it was time to go home.

The moon and stars were hidden by the clouds and on a secluded part of the route to their home they came upon red emergency reflectors that had just been placed on the highway. When they inquired about the trouble they learned that a herd of cows had broken down a fence and was grazing the highway grasses. The entire road was covered with coal black, heavy beasts that would not have been easy to see in the intense darkness. When they arrived on the scene, a car had already struck one of the cows and another vehicle had swerved into a ditch.

Oakley and Lois are convinced that if they had left at the end of their CMA meeting, as was their normal practice, they would have met with disaster on the road home. With an obvious tone of gratitude, Oakley said, "I give God the credit for the protection He gave us that night!" Without a doubt, the specific spot on that Kansas highway will forever remain a memorable site in the souls of the Korbeliks.

It is not a bad idea to physically mark a special place if it can be done subtly enough that it is not vandalism. I personally know it can be rewarding to visit it again or tell others about the place so they can look for it. But for sure, the heart also can be peppered with memories of where God made His goodness known. One of the greatest benefits of recalling those places is the encouragement we find in looking at the mark and reflecting on God's presence in our lives.

"Ebenezers" help us remember who we must go to for the needed strength to keep pressing on!

Blessed be Your name, God, for those times You have helped me through a difficult place. There are so many of them, and You alone are to be praised for such kindness. As I pass by them in my heart, I will pause to say thank You. In Jesus' name, amen.

Let the word of Christ richly dwell within you, with all wisdom teaching and admonishing one another....

Colossians 3:15

20

The Safest Ride

*Do not merely look out for your own personal interests,
but also for the interests of others. Have this attitude in
yourselves which was also in Christ Jesus.*

Philippians 2:4-5

When motorcycles first came on the scene in America, anybody who got to see one considered it an exciting event. But not every person took so quickly to their presence. A case in point is the tale about an elderly couple working outside in the garden near their house. The quiet of the remote hollow where they lived was suddenly filled with a disconcerting rumble. The old man stood upright, then leaned on the long wooden handle of his hoe and peered down through the valley.

In the distance, on the dirt road, he saw a cloud of dust boiling up around a beastly looking thing. The loud noise it was creating as it approached made him feel unsafe. He turned on his heels and sternly instructed his wife, "Get into the house, Sarah. Do it quick. Run!"

The old gentleman closed the door of his home, scurried to his gun cabinet, and retrieved a long-barreled 12-gauge shotgun. He nervously hurried to the window, raised it in time to draw a bead on his target, and emptied a round at the passing creature. The shaken old lady asked, "What was it, Dear?" With a sigh of relief in his voice, her husband answered, "I have no idea. But whatever it was, I made it let go of that man!"

I don't know about you, but I'm glad that motorcycles are a common sight these days! I wouldn't want to be the victim of someone's unfounded fear. Yet, as common as they are, there are still those who would like to separate the machine from its rider. These folks are usually called spouses, family, friends, and generally well-meaning, concerned loved ones.

They have legitimate reasons for wanting to make the beast let go of the man. While some are understandably afraid of the danger that is represented by the ride, this is not the only cause for their dislike of the bike. More often, it is the distraction from important relationships that causes some folks to break out their guns of resistance.

Like anything else that can consume a person, the love of motorcycling can overpower our ability to think clearly in terms of the needs of others. As a hunter, for example, I have to be very careful about how much time I spend in the woods away from family. If I'm not attentive to controlling my "obsession" for pursuing animals such as the whitetail deer, I run the risk of offending my most important *dear*. For that reason, I try to compensate for my time in the deerstand by not neglecting time spent with my wife. Also, if I spend X numbers of dollars on hunting gear, it is only fair that she is free to spend that exact amount on her interests.

The same policies apply to my passion for motorcycling. The amount of time away and money spent can determine how family members will accept or reject my pursuits. My goal is to help my loved ones not resent one moment or one penny I spend on the things I enjoy doing.

I am convinced that this is the way of Christ as described in today's passage. It's not an easy mandate to follow. It goes against the very grain of my human nature. My normal actions are usually based on "selfishness or empty conceit" (Philippians 2:3). However, if I am to gain victory over "the flesh," I must consider what the spirit of Christ would have me do.

For example, I know my wife has tentative feelings about me being so exposed to danger on the unprotected frame of a bike as I career down the highway at the speed limit. Not every woman shares this apprehension, of course, but not every woman is my wife. I have one person I must give serious deference to in regard to such concerns. For that reason, I limit my riding to the safest possible roadways and the least congested times of the day. This concession is quite fair as far as I'm concerned. Annie's not asking me to park the thing and look at it as garage art. She appreciates my interest.

For those who might think I'm a wimp for being so considerate of my wife's fears, I point out that it takes a lot more courage to say no to our desires than to give in to them by ignoring another person's feelings. There are times when I would love to take the most direct route to a place by entering the speedy chaos of a busy interstate highway. Lots of riders do it all the time and feel quite comfortable. However, each relationship has its own unique rules and this is one for me. It is quite satisfying to make this sacrifice for my sweetheart. As a result, she hasn't attempted to shoot my bike out from under me.

I encourage you to take the time to ponder the attitudes that drive your actions with those you love. Are they based on Philippians 2? Or are they based on your reasoning? Remember the passage for today does not imply that you do not have needs. It does not say, "You have no interests." Read it closely and you'll see that it clearly recognizes your interests; however, in order to have the mind of Christ you have been given the grand opportunity of considering others as more important than yourself.

Lord, thank You for those who love me. I want to treat them as You would. Help me see their needs as much more important than my own. And as I meet their needs, I know You'll meet mine. In Jesus' name, amen.

With humility of mind regard one another as more important than yourselves.

Philippians 2:3

21

A Gift Is Still a Gift

As each one has received a special gift,
employ it in serving one another as good stewards
of the manifold grace of God.

1 Peter 4:10

When a human gives a gift, it is usually intended to be enjoyed only by the person to whom it is given. For that reason, the gift changes from a present to a possession the moment it is received. If, for example, my birthday rolls around and my wife gets me a new set of tires for my motorcycle at our local bike shop, they are for me personally. (I hope she reads this!) No one else benefits by it. In turn, when Christmas arrives and I get her a fur coat, it is hers alone to wear and enjoy. (I hope she doesn't read this.)

Things are quite different in the kingdom of God. When God gives a gift to a human, it usually remains just that—a gift to be given away, not a thing to possess. Jesus "summoned His twelve disciples and *gave* them authority over unclean spirits, to cast them out, and to heal every kind of disease and every kind of sickness" (Matthew 10:1, emphasis added). These unbelievable gifts were not put into the disciples' lives for the purpose of admiring and going about showing others what "goodies" God hands out. To the contrary, the men were to turn to those they encountered and pass on the gifts as they began to "heal the sick, raise the dead, cleanse the lepers, cast out demons…" (verse 8). The last part of this verse proves that a gift God gives is not to be held as a possession: "Freely you received, freely give."

Imagine what a loss to the church if John Newton, after writing "Amazing Grace," had decided to sing the song only to himself every morning for devotions. This great anthem of the church would have been tragically hidden in one lone heart. Instead, he lifted his voice and blessed the rest of us with the heavenly gift.

Suppose Billy Graham never braved the pulpit with his marvelous gift of preaching? What if he stood before a mirror and quietly admired the tremendous communication skills God poured into him. What a sad tragedy that would have been for many a lost soul.

The greatest gift of all is proclaimed in John 3:16: "For God so loved the world, that He gave His only begotten Son, that whoever believes in Him shall not perish, but have eternal life." Every one of us who has received Jesus as Savior and Lord has an opportunity to shape the gift that is still a gift when given by the loving hand of God. May we share Jesus with someone today.

Father in heaven, blessed be Your name for the matchless gift of Your Son, Jesus. What an immeasurable sacrifice You made to provide eternal redemption for me. May it never be that I silently hold to the joy. I will gladly and boldly pass on the gift of Your Son. In Jesus' name, amen.

**[I] implore you to walk in a manner
worthy of the calling with which you have been called,
with all humility and gentleness, showing tolerance
for one another in love, being diligent to preserve
the unity of the Spirit in the bond of peace.**

Ephesians 4:1-3

22

Dirt & Spit

Therefore they said to him, "How were your eyes opened?"
John 9:10

It's not easy to make a U-turn on a very narrow, Tennessee back road with a heavy motorcycle. But, with considerable maneuvering I managed to do it. Then I discovered that the half-foot shoulder of the road was not an ideal parking spot, especially in a curve. However, with enough careful throttling I was able to get off the pavement and into the knee-high grass. Why all the effort? Blackberries!

I got a quick glimpse of them as I slowly rounded the bend, and I knew I had to partake. They were thumb-size and plump with juice. I dismounted, and with my eye on the weeds as a lookout for pesky snakes, pressed through to the thorny vines that were heavy with one of my favorite summer foods.

I spent at least ten minutes reaching over and under and through the sharp points of the thorns. I didn't pick a berry unless it felt soft to the touch and released easily from the vine. Those that even slightly held on were a tad bit premature and were left to continue ripening.

Feeling quite satisfied with having eaten the equivalent of five heaping handfuls of berries, I headed back to my bike. As I stood on the roadside enjoying the aftertaste and picking the little residual seeds out of my teeth, I leaned over to take a look in my rearview mirrors to see how deep the purplish-blue color was on my tongue. It looked just like the same tongue that had been stained many years ago when I used to invade the berry patches as a kid.

Before I put my helmet back on I decided to see (sorry ladies) how dark my spit was. I gathered up a more than conservative amount in my mouth and let it fly toward the sandy edge of the road. The sugar/saliva mixture held together in a nice, tumbling, oblong clump as it descended to the ground.

When the odd-shaped liquid ball landed at a 45-degree angle, it did what I've seen the watery wads do all through my life. It slid along the surface of the dust and collected enough of it to immediately make a small ball of mud. I sort of chuckled out loud at myself when I realized there was still plenty of little boy left in me to be intrigued by such a sight.

It was a little ways down the road when I thought of a biblical similarity between the mud ball I had created and another one mentioned in John 9. Jesus stopped by a man who had been blind since birth. After a brief conversation about sin, Jesus "spat on the ground, and made clay of the spittle, and applied the clay to his eyes" (verse 6). Then the man was instructed to "wash in the pool of Siloam." When the blind man returned from this unusual procedure, he could see!

Several gems of truth can be mined from this story. Jesus had just told his disciples, "While I am in the world, I am the Light of the world." To illustrate this truth, he chose a blind man who had not seen the light of even a single day of his existence to reveal what happens when Jesus comes into a life. The man's obedience to the Lord's instructions about going to the pool and washing is a great testimony to the value of doing exactly as He says, even if what He requires seems absurd to the rest of the world. And, as already mentioned, Jesus used this opportunity to teach about sin. This entire situation became God's opportunity to display Himself to the inquisitive disciples, to the blind man, to the blind man's neighbors, and to everyone else present.

All those nuggets of hope and insight centered around a little spit and dust. There are undoubtedly more truths to be gleaned from this episode, but the most encouraging thought, as far as I'm concerned, is that I am but dust...but add Jesus...and miracles can happen. Blessed be His name!

Jesus, thank You for letting me witness Your encounter with the blind man. Never is anything You do less than majestic! Even when You spat on the ground it was royal spit. I praise You for being willing to add Yourself to my life of clay. In Your name, amen.

So he went away and washed, and came back seeing.

John 9:7

23

Grandma Could Have Been a Biker

So we speak, not as pleasing men,
but God who examines our hearts.

1 Thessalonians 2:4

My maternal Grandmother Steel would have made a classic—and classy—motorcyclist. I don't say this because of any interest she revealed in bikes or because she had an adventurous spirit. I make this statement because she was the type of person who was not commonly swayed by the opinions of others.

For example, if someone were to ask her, "Mrs. Steel, are you going to church tonight?" though her answer most of the time would have been an affirmative, there were times when she would reply with a simple no. If the inquisitor pursued her about her choice to forsake the assembling with the saints, my grandma would not soft sell her response with a halfhearted untruth. Instead, her answer to the person's query would be a firm, "'Cause I don't want to!"

As the chips fell where they may, my sweet grandma would go about her business unconcerned about the impression that might have been left in the mind of the one who had challenged her choice to stay home. Grandma Steel possessed the attitude described in today's verse. My grandmother opted for honesty, which pleases God. I deeply admired her for that trait, and it inspires me to be the same.

Most motorcyclists I know are like my grandma. By nature, they are not overly concerned with the opinions of too many others. If they are fans of helmetless riding, that's just the way it will be (if state law allows it). If they like extra chrome or a plain Jane, a front fender or no fender, a windshield or the wind, face mask or open, it is typical that no matter what others say, the bikers aren't usually affected by it.

Any person who is confident enough to ignore the temptation to always seek the best opinion of themselves from the lips of others is a person who can make a great follower of Christ. Ingrained in their basic personality is a willingness to press on in the face of scoffing. These types of individuals can be "approved by God to be entrusted with the gospel," a message that is not necessarily loved by every hearer, as pointed out in 1 Corinthians 1:23: "We preach Christ crucified, to Jews a stumbling block and to Gentiles foolishness."

It takes a brave soul to fend off the tendency to be a human-pleaser. My grandma was one of them; some of my biking friends are too. I want to be courageous enough to do so as well that I may be bold in sharing the gospel of Jesus Christ. How about you? How would you answer the question in Galatians 1:10: "For am I now seeking the favor of men, or of God?"

Should the opportunity come today to speak of You and Your Holy Son, Jesus, thank You even now for the courage to do so. I want to please You! In Jesus' name, amen.

...If I were still trying to please men,
I would not be a bond-servant of Christ.

Galatians 1:10

24

Apostle Paul and Mr. Honda

*Most gladly, therefore, I will rather boast
about my weaknesses, so that the power
of Christ may dwell in me.*

2 Corinthians 12:9

Mr. Soichiro Honda, the man responsible for the founding of Honda (as in motorcycles) was initially far less than the successful entrepreneur he turned out to be. In his own words he offers a description of his life: "Nothing but mistakes, a series of failures, a series of regrets."

It is interesting that such a notable figure in the business world, when asked to put the spotlight on the part of his past that held the most meaning, would direct the beam to his failures. But he had a reason for doing it, which is revealed in his own admission: "Success can be achieved only through repeated failure and introspection. In fact, success represents the 1 percent of your work that results from 99 percent that is called failure."

Mr. Honda's candid statement has a familiar ring to it. In his willingness to recognize that it is in the soil of defeat that victory can grow, I hear the echoes of a portion of the apostle Paul's letter to the Corinthians: "On my own behalf I will not boast, except in regard to my weakness" (2 Corinthians 12:5).

Keep in mind that Paul was speaking to a braggadocios people when he addressed the Corinthians. Seldom does the apostle even consider bragging in the New Testament. In fact, when he wrote earlier in the chapter, "I know a man in Christ who...was caught up to the third heaven... caught up into Paradise and heard inexpressible words, which a man is not permitted to speak" (verses 2,4), Paul was referring to himself. His refusal to forsake humility in order to boast is evident in the way he spoke of himself in the third person.

The Corinthians, however, were known to "talk up" their spiritual gifts and visions. Apparently Paul felt they were becoming so heavenly minded that they were losing their earthly effectiveness. Consequently, he tried to help them keep a balance between their spiritual and natural lives. He wanted them to be realistic about their humanness while they experienced the "superterrestrial." In order to gain their respect for his authority and so they'd listen to his corrective instructions, Paul found it necessary to engage in a little boasting about his unique visit to heaven. He was sure that if he sufficiently impressed them they would be more open to accepting the fact that when it came to spiritual matters he knew what he was talking about.

Paul prefaces his remarks about his own experiences by asserting that although boasting was necessary in their case, it was not especially profitable (verse 1). His serious dislike of having to do so was clear in his words in verse 11: "I have become foolish; you yourselves compelled me." With that indictment he quickly pointed the Corinthians to the real cause for any of his spiritual success that might have given them reason for awe. He declared, "Therefore I am well content with weakness, with insults, with distresses, with persecutions, with difficulties, for Christ's sake; for when I am weak, then I am strong" (2 Corinthians 12:10).

Paul understood something that even Mr. Honda, whether he embraced the God of the apostle or not, found to be the right way to view one's shortcomings. When people recognize their weaknesses and failures, then they know they must go elsewhere for strength and success. In Paul's case, as it can and should be for the rest of us, he went to God. He lifted his cup of weakness to heaven, and the Lord poured His power into it.

What are you bragging about today?

Father, thank You for the times I have had to come to You with my failures. And thank You for lending me successes that are made even sweeter because it was in my weakness that Your might was made obvious. Lead me and use me even when I feel powerless, because I know You'll supply what I need and the result will be that You'll get the glory. In Jesus' name, amen.

Let him who boasts, boast in the LORD.

1 Corinthians 1:31

25

Biking in the Dark

*The light shines in the darkness,
and the darkness did not comprehend it.*

John 1:5

If you've ever been cruising along through the night and suddenly your head lamp goes out, you know how precious light can be. As your eyes instantly attempt to adjust and try to look through the black wall, you tentatively hit the brakes and try to remember whether or not there was a curve ahead. The temptation to panic is unbelievably strong. As the mind scrambles for solutions, the body tightens up and the spirit cries out for divine protection.

Having had my own "lights out" experience, I have to ask: "How could people intentionally allow themselves to fall into the category of the folks mentioned in John 3:19? That verse says, "...and men loved the darkness rather than the light." Loved darkness? It is beyond my comprehension why anyone would embrace the uncertainties of the absence of light. Physically speaking, I don't care that much for operating in it at any speed, even with a headlight. When my body is being hurled like a projectile at 55 or 60 miles per hour, I *want* illumination, at minimum enough to have advance warning about obstacles such as rocks, rusty bumpers, possums, or sand and gravel that may have washed up onto the pavement. It's tough enough to enlist a nimble reaction to such things in the daytime; at night, with the sight distance reduced drastically, it is even more of a challenge.

I suppose if I had a love affair with pain, I wouldn't wait for my headlight to go out. Instead, I would reach over my handlebars with my Leatherman and punch a hole in the lamp glass. Then I'd have all the darkness I wanted. Doesn't that sound foolish to you?

It sounds just as odd, spiritually speaking, that someone would choose darkness rather than light. But if it's evil deeds that he or she enjoys doing, then that explains the affection for the night—it's a cover for sin.

Those who embrace righteousness and pursue it will be consummate lovers of light. They'll desire it like their bellies long for food to eat. They'll cherish it the way I care for the headlamp mounted to the front of my bike. Without it, disaster is sure. I *want* my headlight, and I want it working! But even more, I want Christ to shine in my life.

Lord, I sincerely thank You for the miracle of light. How it guides and comforts is a blessing both to my body and my soul. May I never be among those who love the darkness. Help me be a light to them so that their affection might change from loving evil to loving You. In Jesus' name, amen.

I am the Light of the world.
John 8:12

26

Splitting the Lanes

*For the gate is small and
the way is narrow that leads to life.*

Matthew 7:14

Splitting the lanes" is a choice some brave motorcyclists make when they want to negotiate through traffic that is either moving extremely slow or stalled. Motoring in that narrow space between two lines of vehicles or two rigs must be done at the lowest speed possible and with great care. The risk is that other vehicles may pull into the biker's path or someone may decide to open a door for some reason. However, if done correctly and lawfully, the beauty of splitting the lane is that it can be a real time-saver.

The advantage of a skinny cycle also includes parking lots, especially when hundreds of cars are waiting to leave a function. Once, after a stock car race, I was in a heavy bottleneck that had developed at our local speedway. Attitudes were beginning to succumb to a day in the heat and thoughts were being exchanged through car horns. (Thankfully, the horns didn't speak English!)

About the time I was ready to pull out of line, park, and wait in order to save some precious fuel in my pickup, I noticed several motorcycles gathered in a corner at the far end of the massive lot. One by one, and rather stealthily I might add, they were passing through a narrow opening in the fence. Each of the riders seemed to be smiling as they waved goodbye to the logjam of cars behind them. *Brilliant!* I thought, as I wished I had ridden my bike to the race.

The memory of that sight came back to me one Sunday when our pastor was delivering a sermon based on Matthew 7:13: "Enter through the narrow gate; for the gate is wide and the way is broad that leads to destruction, and there are many who enter through it." He pointed out that in order to pass through a narrow opening, a person can't be burdened down with a lot of excess baggage. He must be streamlined, even stripped of all worldly attachments, before he can fit through the tight confines of a narrow passageway.

Laying aside the bulkiness of things such as the lust of the flesh, the pride of life, greed, gossip, ungodly entertainment, and the elevation of self above others is part of initiating a relationship with Jesus. Entering into the narrow gate requires a repentant heart and complete surrender to Him.

How does a person accomplish the task of casting off the things that hinder his passage through the gate? The answer is found in the truth contained in a statement my pastor made that Sunday: "Salvation is a free gift of God that costs us everything!" As an example of the sacrifices we must be willing to make in order to follow the Lord, the pastor pointed to Luke 14:26. That verse challenges all those who come to Christ that they must be willing to love Him more than they love their very own families. That, my friend, is the ultimate in making ourselves spiritually slender!

Perhaps you have considered completely surrendering your life to the Lord. Yet when you attempt to come to Him there may be something that keeps you from getting through. Could it be that your "vehicle" is too wide? Is it possible that this is true because you have loaded too many things on it? Even a thin motorcycle can become too broad for a narrow opening if too much is packed on it. Whatever the excess baggage might be, may God bless you as you allow Him to help you spiritually split the lanes and make your way to Him.

Father in heaven, thank You for the gift of Your Son, Jesus. I acknowledge that He alone is the way to You. I want to be in Your sweet presence. Show me the things I need to cast off in order to draw closer to You. Give me the strength and courage to do them. In Jesus' name, amen.

Strive to enter through the narrow door; for many, I tell you, will seek to enter and will not be able.

Luke 13:24

27

Who Hit Whom?

Therefore, confess your sins to one another, and pray for one another so that you may be healed.

James 5:16

Can you identify the following creature using these hints?

> Sound: A crunchy splat
>
> Sight: A teardrop-shaped, flat spray in colors ranging from a dull to brilliant yellow, muted to bright reds, and an occasional purplish green
>
> Comment: "He'll never have the guts to do that again!"

I'm sure the last hint gave it away. The answer is a bug. Sometimes when I take my helmet off and see the sizable juicy remains of what was an insect, I wonder what kind of welt would have been on my head if it had not been protected. I've wiped some really gross messes off my headgear and my windshield. As I clean the bike parts that have connected violently with the poor vermin, there have been a few times I have actually felt sorrow for the unfortunate things. After all, they didn't get in my way. To say "a bug hit my windshield" is misrepresenting the truth. The fact is, I hit the bug with my windshield. I invaded its territory; it didn't trespass upon mine.

I think we should have a national campaign that reeducates all citizens about this issue so that we will feel the pain that surely the bug community experiences. For much too long, the responsibility for these crimes against nature has been unjustly placed on the wrong party. The real question is, "Who hit whom?" I say it's high time for some convictions and sentences to be handed down to the ones who are really at fault. Surely there is juicetice…I mean justice for bugs.

Jokes about their demise should be stopped. No more "what went through its mind in that moment? Glass!" (or plastic if the murder weapon was a motorcycle). It doesn't seem right that so much fun is had at the expense of these innocent "flystanders," er, "by-flyers."

Okay I got a little carried away with this "matter." It's hard to resist the levity that is normally connected to the bonk of a bug on a windshield. But as insignificant as it seems, there is a valuable analogy that can be gleaned from a bug's sad ending. It came to me when my vision was nearly blocked by the death spray of a monster bug on my face shield.

I immediately blamed the bug for the layer of litter on my helmet. I groaned, "That stupid thing did this to me!" I was livid as I stopped my cruising and searched for a gas station where I could grab some paper towels.

Isn't it interesting how we are also so willing to pass the bug—er, buck, by blaming others for the colorful crust that dirties our emotional windshields? But isn't it in our nature to do just that? The first man, Adam, set the pace for the rest of us when he blamed Eve for his indulgence in the fruit of the tree that God said to leave alone. His attempt to put the responsibility for his infamous sin on the back of his wife is a well-known story to just about everyone.

To not "own" our failures and faults is to avoid the work God wants to do in our hearts. By laying claim to the times we are the guilty ones, the first thing we do is open the door to the marvelous interaction of human repentance and divine forgiveness. The incredible inner peace that follows is honey to the spirit.

By owning our transgressions against others, we remove the element of bitterness that can sour relationships. With the foul taste of blame removed, two individuals can feel free to forgive and forget instead of resent and resist. Imagine what the outcome would have been if Adam would have said, "I ate the fruit. I'm guilty!"

The next time you hear the unmistakable sound of *your* windshield hitting a bug, remember who's to blame. Let it remind you to own your guilt—then at least the bug's life would not have ended in vain.

Father, thank You for Your forgiveness for sin. Help me never use blame as a way of avoiding my own guilt. I need Your grace today to make things right with those I have wrongly blamed. As I do, I trust that You will clean the splats from my heart. In Jesus' name, amen.

If we confess our sins, He is faithful and
righteous to forgive us our sins and
to cleanse us from all unrighteousness.

1 John 1:9

28

The Ride of Your Life

...to love the LORD your God, to walk in all His ways and hold fast to Him.

Deuteronomy 11:22

I'll never forget November 1995. Annie and I had just completed a Bible study that focused on knowing the will of God. The timing of the study was undoubtedly divine because it was very soon after finishing the class that both our hearts began to sense a very real "stirring." Each of us independently felt our lives were going to experience significant changes. We had no idea how true it would be. Within a mere three months, life went from a casual, relaxed ride to careening at rocket speed down the highway of change. Selling our house, moving, switching churches, and starting a new company were just the beginning of a whirlwind of change to our once-peaceful lives.

We look back now and see that the unsettledness that we felt prior to our upheaval was God's Spirit warning us to brace ourselves for what was ahead. His quiet prompting was a little like what our son heard when he took a motorcycle ride with our friend, Gary Heddon.

Gary's getaway from the rigors of being a well-respected and sought-after technician in the world of audio engineering is his BMW bike. Nothing seems to push the refresh button on his mental computer better than a 20-minute cruise down the highway near his home.

Nathan was in the studio with Gary as he was doing some final mastering of a recording project for us. When he had reached the peak of data intake and signal manipulation, Gary said to our son, "Let's give our brains a break and go for a Beemer ride." Nathan agreed and off they went. As they carefully maneuvered over the gravel road toward the pavement, Nathan had his hands gently draped over his pilot's shoulders. Knowing what was ahead for his passenger, Gary turned his head and spoke just loud enough through his helmet for Nathan to hear, "You might want to hold on tighter than that!"

Not knowing about the power of the engine that smoothly rumbled under his seat, Nathan didn't understand what was about to happen. He reported that when Gary rolled the throttle of his bike the acceleration was unbelievable. Just in time, he grabbed his driver by the waist and managed to avoid getting dumped onto the road. He said the ride was beyond thrilling and that the excited, uncontrollable yell in the confines of his helmet nearly burst his own eardrums.

Gary's wise warning to his unsuspecting passenger is a clear illustration of what God may be offering you this very moment. Perhaps there's a stirring in your soul about a matter. You sense change ahead. Maybe something about your life is about to be altered...big time. That awareness could be your heavenly Father gently letting you know that the relaxed hold you have on Him is not going to be enough when the acceleration of changes comes.

How do we strengthen our hold on Him? Pray—pray hard; pray longer. Fast more often. Read God's Word, not the world. Meditate on the Bible's truths. And, most important, trust your divine driver. If He has said to tighten your grip, embrace Him like you never have before! Like Nathan trusted Gary, you can surely trust God during the ride of your life.

Father, thank You that I can trust You with my journey. Help me always be willing to tighten my embrace of Your guidance. I don't want to be left behind when You move ahead. In Jesus' name, amen.

Draw near to God and He will draw near to you.

James 4:8

29

The Triumph

When He had disarmed the rulers and authorities,
He made a public display of them, having triumphed
over them through Him.

Colossians 2:15

When I was stationed on the aircraft carrier *USS Forrestal/CVA-59* in 1971–72, we made a six-month Mediterranean cruise. During our time away from the states, something happened at one of the ports in the Mediterranean that I thought was interesting and very thoughtful of the ship's captain.

I'll never forget the scene as the boat's cranes dropped to the dock and loaded up several wooden crates containing partially assembled Triumph motorcycles. As they were hoisted into the belly of the massive ship, their excited owners watched with gratitude as their prizes were stored along the outer hull inside the hangar bay. With a nervous laughter, these guys chattered among themselves, hardly able to contain the anticipation of getting back to home soil with their brand-new bikes.

At that time I was not a biker, but I do recall noticing the distinguishable logo of the Triumph that was burned into the side of the wooden crates. The artistic shape of the name was very inviting. But what was more appealing to the ones who would eventually mount the machines was the price they paid for them. Their investment was quite manageable on a sailor's meager wage because two things were eliminated: the shipping and assembling. Literally hundreds of dollars were saved because the captain cared about his men and let them bring the bikes on board.

Though I've never owned a Triumph, to this day I enjoy seeing one. The sight of it brings back the memory of the faces of my shipmates who were glowing with utter joy when they stood around the crates and talked of the good times to come.

Besides liking the sight of a Triumph, I love to hear the name. It reminds me of one of my favorite words in the Scriptures. One particular place it appears is 2 Corinthians 2:14: "But thanks be to God, who always leads us in triumph in Christ." The word "triumph" oozes with the comforting report of victory. I almost want to raise my hand with a wave of joy each time I say it in relation to Jesus' mighty work.

There's an obvious difference between the two "triumphs." While my fellow sailors got theirs relatively cheap, the triumph over sin and death that Christ obtained for us cost Him His life. Paul tells about this great sacrifice in his letter to the Romans: "But God demonstrates His own love toward us, in that while we were yet sinners, Christ died for us" (5:8).

What a marvelous gift God has given us in His Son! In Him, we will always know triumph.

Oh blessed Savior, thank You from the bottom of my once sin-stained heart for the incredible sacrifice You made to give me victory over the deadly, eternal effects of my transgressions. I bless Your holy name and pray for Your strength and boldness to always live so that my life gives You the glory you deserve. In Jesus' triumphant name, amen.

Victory belongs to the LORD.
Proverbs 21:31

30

Just a Vapor

Yet you do not know what your life will be like tomorrow.
You are just a vapor that appears for a little while and
then vanishes away.

James 4:14

About as fast as telephone poles march by me while I'm
motoring down a country highway, that's the way the
years seem to have gone by. It is as though mere seconds
have passed between the more noticeable annual events
like birthdays, Christmas and Easter, and the first day of
deer season. Today, the memorable happenings that I
thought would never arrive, such as high-school gradua-
tion, my wedding day, and the births of my children, are
now precious moments stored side by side on a special
shelf in my heart. Amazingly, because not one minute
separates them now, I can look back through time and
enjoy each and every memory in rapid succession.

In an attempt to describe the similarity between a
man's existence and disappearing vapor, I penned the following sonnet:

A Life in a Day

I crawled from my crib
  this morning
Went in and shaved
  my face

This afternoon I said,
   "Dear wife, don't we have a
   lovely place"
This evening all
   my children
Gather 'round me
   one last time
Tonight I lay me down to rest
     in a crib of fancy pine.

Depressing, but true, isn't it? Knowing that my book is in the hands of time and that he's reading much too fast, I am compelled to not waste the minutes that have been put into my account of days. To do so would be as foolish as a gold digger throwing away the valuable nuggets that fill his pull-string bag. Each one has immense value and should not be discarded unwisely.

I want to live with a heart tuned to God's will, to look for the way He wants to use me and redeem my time. And, in this world that has been made cold because of sin, I want the "vapor of breath that I am" to form the name of Christ so that others will see it and find hope and warmth.

God, thank You for every minute You have breathed into my life. In the short moment of time that I appear in this world, make it so that others will see You in it. In Jesus' name, amen.

My times are in Your hand....

Psalm 31:15

31

The Hub

*Therefore if there is any encouragement
in Christ, if there is any consolation of love,
if there is any fellowship of the Spirit, if any affection
and compassion, make my joy complete by being
of the same mind, maintaining the same love,
united in spirit, intent on one purpose.*

Philippians 2:1-2

Did you know the answer to all your family's problems is found on your motorcycle? That's right! The picture of how to have a healthy home is closer than you think. Where is it? In your wheels.

Not long before Annie and I married, a gentleman gave us some advice regarding our relationship that is, to this day, how we strive to live. Using an illustration of a wagon wheel as his teaching device (a bike wheel provides the same picture), he said, "Steve, make your family look like this wagon wheel. Put Christ at the hub of your home. And you, as individuals, follow the line of the spokes to the hub. As each of you are pursuing Christ, moving toward Him like the spokes in this wheel, you will draw closer to one another through the years." He concluded with a tone of confidence I will never forget, "I can give you a full guarantee that this works." He was right!

After more than a quarter of a century of marriage, I have come to understand why the wise gentleman's advice has been so effective. When two people in a relationship individually allow the Spirit of God to draw them to His ways as prescribed in the Scriptures, they cease to be preoccupied with the deadliest of poisons that can slowly kill a relationship—the self. Because their deepest desire is to please the Lord in all they say and do, they are not dependent on fickle human love to sustain them. They are always refreshed by the divine love of Christ that flows through them.

As an example of how the "spokes in the wheel" method works according to the Scriptures, Philippians 2:3 is a good place to look: "Do nothing from selfishness or empty conceit, but with humility of mind regard one another as more important than yourselves." Notice that the passage *does not* say that one is important and the other is not. To the contrary, it clearly recognizes that *both* parties have value. However, when one sees the other as more important, then he or she is allowing the Spirit of our Savior to influence their relationship. "Have this attitude in yourselves which was also in Christ Jesus" (verse 5).

The moment two people start moving in the single direction of maintaining this godly mindset, they instantly begin drawing closer in their own hearts to each other. And if there are new spokes added to the wheel (children), and they are also taught to join in on the journey to the hub, the entire family will find joy in dwelling together.

May the Lord bless you as you ride today. And the next time you check your tire pressure, may you notice the hub of your wheel and be reminded to offer up a prayer for your home.

Father in heaven, thank You for the relationships You have given me with those I love. I invite You to first occupy my

heart. Help me to pursue You daily, to learn of You through Your Word, to think like You and to act like You. I invite You to enter into my family's dynamics. Like the hub of a wheel, be at the center of my home. I pray for strength and courage for each member of my family to have Your attitude and pursue You so that as we draw closer to You, we'll draw closer to those around us. I pray for those who are not yet on the journey to You. Help me know what to say to them and how to serve them in a way that testifies to the joy of knowing You. And until You come, draw me close to You. In Jesus' name, amen.

Do not merely look out for your own personal interests, but also for the interests of others.

Philippians 2:4

32

Daditude

Truly, truly, I say to you, the Son can do nothing of Himself, unless it is something He sees the Father doing.

John 5:19

In the month of February 2001, the world of motorsports lost a great talent. Dale Earnhardt was (and still is) one of the most well-respected figures in auto racing. When his life ended so suddenly at the Daytona 500, every race fan fell silent.

Perhaps the most heart-wrenching sight was the live coverage of the moment his son, Dale Jr., still in his driver's suit, walked into the hospital emergency room where his father had been taken. The man he so loved, who had taught him everything he knew about driving skills, was already gone. The sadness was excruciating. It was a solemn day to say the very least.

Five short months later, in July, Dale Jr. returned to the Daytona Speedway to race again. That night the emotional pendulum took a swing all the way to the opposite side of February's sorrowful memory. In the style of his late father, young Dale was leading the pack when the checkered flag was lifted at the end of the 400-mile contest. The crowd went absolutely wild with happiness that the legendary Earnhardt name would be carved once again into a trophy that was presented in the winner's lane. I was among those who were grinning from ear to ear.

Following Dale's win, some vicious rumors were started about whether or not there might have been some technical advantage given to his car by the NASCAR organization. These unfair and inaccurate reports were based on the sentimental element of the race. When asked about his feelings regarding the unfortunate hearsay, Dale Jr.'s response was classic. It was stated something like this, "Well, I guess we'll have to wait till the next [expletive] whoopin' to see if what they're sayin' is true!" Though I don't approve of his choice of words, I understand his emotion. Furthermore, his fervor had a familiar ring to it.

Apparently a local TV sportscaster felt the same thing I did when he heard Dale Jr.'s statement. His commentary on the young intimidator's tenacity was unforgettable. When the camera came back to him he looked over at his coreporter and said, "Now, that's what I call a daditude!"

Dale Earnhardt Sr. was known for his unbridled passion for winning races. He did not hide his feelings under the sheet metal of his car. Known for the way he wrestled his way to the front time after time through the years, Dale Sr. gave everyone who was watching the race the best return for their hard-earned entertainment dollar. I have a feeling the same will eventually be said of his incredibly gifted son.

I think it would be great if people said that I have a daditude! My father is also worthy to imitate. He doesn't drive race cars (although I'm confident he would love to try his hand at it!). He has never made the front of a newspaper sports page, nor does he have shelves full of trophies that testify to track intimidation. However, he does have in him the Spirit of our holy God. Something of far greater value!

My dad is gentle, wise, loving, compassionate, honest, and has a compelling desire to lead others to Christ. With so many attributes in his favor, if I can be like him in just a small way, I know I will have done well. I am far more proud of my dad's spiritual accomplishments than any son could ever be of a dad who has excelled in worldly pursuits. Why? If I am like him I will ultimately be like my heavenly Father, who has filled my earthly dad's heart with His presence. Also, all the temporal exploits that a man can boast of do not hold a candle to the everlasting triumph of knowing and living for Christ. By yielding his life to the Lord, my dad has done the greatest feat. His trophies are sure, and they wait for him on heaven's shelves. I want to be like him.

I sincerely hope and pray that my son, Nathan, will also be accused of daditude. O, Lord, may it be!

Father, I am eternally grateful that You have made me one of Your own through the gift of Your beloved Son, Jesus. Help me live for You in such a way that my children will want to be like You. In Jesus' name, amen.

For whatever the Father does, these things
the Son also does in like manner.

John 5:19

33

Riding Staggered

*Only conduct yourselves in a manner
worthy of the gospel of Christ.*
Philippians 1:27

One of the well-known rules of the road for motor-cyclists who travel together is to ride in a staggered formation. The space and distance this method of group movement offers to the biker is important for his personal safety as well as the safety of those around him. Riding in a pack front to back, side by side, poses a great hazard if the person in front suddenly hits the brakes. The extra second or two of maneuvering or stopping time that staggered riding provides can mean the difference between highway happiness and road rash!

As any biker knows, it takes steady concentration to ride in a staggered formation. Not much time is allowed for catching the sights of the territory. Undivided attention is the main ingredient for a successful motorcade of cycles. Each rider must work out his or her own ride. A certain healthy respect for the situation is at the forefront of the rider's mind.

That concept, whenever I hear it or see it, reminds me of a passage of Scripture that speaks to the importance of each Christian tending to his or her own walk with Christ. It is found in Philippians 2:12 NKJV: "Therefore, my beloved, as you have always obeyed, not as in my presence only, but now much more in my absence, work out your own salvation with fear and trembling."

It was one thing for the Philippians to follow Christ when Paul was with them in person, when his presence inspired them to holiness. When he was no longer around, they had to call on their own motivation to be faithful to their lives of righteousness. It must have been unsettling for them to "go it alone," yet that is exactly what Paul is calling them to do.

Those of us who follow Christ today are not unlike the Philippians of the Bible. We, too, must give our utmost attention to our personal journey with the Lord. And there's a good reason for it! Just like a motorcyclist riding in a group who allows himself to be distracted by the world around him and causes others to tumble, we as Christians must be careful about our own spiritual integrity. To be enticed by the world and get off track is to run the risk of hurting ourselves and injuring others.

One of the most obvious examples of how a person's choices can affect others is found in King David's sexual sin with Bathsheba (see 1 Samuel). By giving into the deadly distraction of his lustful desire for her, he set into motion horrific events. From deviously orchestrating lives to arranging the murder of Uriah (Bathsheba's husband), the king attempted to cover up his adultery. The consequential death of his first son born to Bathsheba was one of the long-term prices David (and Bathsheba) paid. How much better it would have been if he had tended to his own "ride" more carefully.

I'll never forget the uneasy feeling I had when I first rode in a group. I felt the necessary isolation one must have, yet I also felt very much part of the unit. Although it was fun, I admit I was nervous when I realized the awesome responsibility I had. I knew very well that my every action could affect the rest of the bunch. As seriously as I took my role in that ride, and in others like it, my own walk with Christ is even more crucial. I know I must do all I can to maintain a position that shows I am following my Lord and leading others to Him as well. May your next group ride bring this truth back to your mind. I hope you enjoy the trip *and* model Jesus to those around you!

Father in heaven, thank You for all those You have put me with on this highway of life. Help me to not be a cause for trouble in their lives by judging how they journey. I want to focus on my relationship with You and how I can be a blessing to others. I praise You for the many times You have protected us from each other. In Jesus' name, amen.

It is God who is at work in you, both to will
and to work for His good pleasure.

Philippians 2:13

34

A Strange Language

*But ye are a chosen generation, a royal priesthood, an
holy nation, a peculiar people.*

1 Peter 2:9 KJV

One day I stood in a bike shop and enjoyed some conversation with a few other motorcycle owners. As I listened to the words we were using, such as "decreasing" and "increasing radius corners," and "belt-drive" and "shaft-drive" systems, I suddenly realized that if a nonbiker were present, he or she would have no clue as to what was being said. While the language barrier bikers create with their uncommon usage of words makes them an odd lot, this uniqueness is not limited to the world of cycling.

All my life I have been around "churched" people. One of the interesting things about growing up in West Virginia in the constant environment of local saints was that I learned to understand the meanings that were often hidden in their vernacular. I essentially took them for granted, and I honestly didn't understand how strange our words and phrases might seem to those who were not familiar with "Christianese." "Getting saved," for example, is understood by nearly all church members as the term for gaining eternal salvation through believing in Christ as Lord and Savior and accepting His sacrifice. In Acts 2:21, the text quotes Joel 2:32, which highlights this essential step: "And it shall be that everyone who calls on the name of the LORD will be saved." Then there's the cry of the jailer who feared for his life when Paul and Silas were miraculously freed from prison by an unexpected earthquake: "Sirs, what must I do to be saved?" (Acts 16:30). Even though believers love the sound of this cry that has been used as a plea for pardon from their transgressions, a person who has never heard the term might ask, "Get saved from what?"

Another curious saying is, "he fell under conviction." While most spiritual pilgrims know this statement refers to the sudden realization a person comes to regarding his or her sinful state, which leads to an awareness of the need for redemption, others might not grasp the idea so quickly. Instead, they may assume a criminal procedure was underway.

One other phrase that always seemed normal to me that an "outsider" might find confusing is "freewill offering." The meaning of this well-used word combination is not a mystery to any of us who have sat in the pews through the years and have cheerfully contributed to the work of the church with our money (as well as other possessions). This phrase has its roots in the first chapter of the book of Ezra: "All those about them encouraged them with articles of silver, with gold, with goods, with cattle, and with valuables, aside from all that was given as a freewill offering" (verse 6).

For those of us who not only walk with Christ but also ride with Him, it is important to recognize that our language may require some interpretation from time to time. With that in mind, be sensitive to who you're talking to and offer explanations for some of the spiritual terms Christians use. This might even provide some great talking points to get a conversation going about the Lord!

In no way am I suggesting that we change our terminology. That would not serve the joy of being a "peculiar people." To alter the unique language that surrounds the kingdom of God would erase one of the differences that needs to exist. What good would it do to so blend with the world that we are not recognizable? For that reason, I proudly commend our strange vernacular and say with a hearty approval, "Press on with the words of the cross!" While doing so, check the expressions of those who listen. If their faces seem suddenly puzzled, it is very possible that the door has just opened to introduce them to a new realm of hope. His name is Jesus!

Thank You, Holy Father, for providing new words of the faith. Each time I use them they remind me that I'm part of a people set apart for Your use. Help me be mindful of those who need You, and give me wisdom about how to tell them of Your great love for them. In Jesus' name, amen.

A peculiar people; that ye should show forth the praises of him who hath called you out of darkness into his marvelous light.

1 Peter 2:9 KJV

35

Spiritual Health Benefits

For bodily exercise profits a little....
I Timothy 4:8

I tend to be obsessive about things. For example, when I was around the age of 30 I decided I would begin a regimen of jogging—strictly to stay in shape. When people furrowed their brows and inquired, "Why do you do it?" I would quote James Dobson's reason for exercising: "So I'll look good in my casket!"

The problem with starting a program of jogging was that I refused to be satisfied with an every-other-day deal. I began with the goal of keeping a strong heart; however, because of my "all out" nature, I went headlong into it. Within a few months I was on my way to pounding the pavement on a daily basis with long runs reaching upwards of ten miles each time out. But my obsessive approach had a price.

About three months after I turned 40 and many half-marathons (and one full marathon) later, I blew a knee. I had a chest-of-drawers full of T-shirts to prove I had participated in the races, but I no longer had a sufficient amount of cartilage under my right kneecap to allow further collections of cotton trophies.

Though I am now limited to the number of miles and the speed at which I can jog/hobble, I have not given up trying to stay in reasonable shape even though my 50-year-old body pretty much dictates the restrictions. I used to sweat *with* the oldies; now I sweat *as* an oldie. But at least I can still sweat!

While today's Scripture is true, it might be that too much exercise is not the issue. Instead, it may be high time to start a program. Note that the verse does not say, "For bodily exercise profits *nothing.*" To the contrary, the passage clearly implies there is *some* benefit to be gained from disciplining the body with exercise. Too many times this verse is taken as a way of escape from engaging in the not-so-pleasant task of working off the pounds.

Although I can personally attest to the importance of maintaining moderation with exercise, I also highly recommend that 1 Corinthians 6:19 be taken seriously by those of us who are ambassadors of Christ. The verse admonishes: "Do you not know that your body is a temple of the Holy Spirit who is in you, whom you have from God, and that you are not your own?"

These words of wisdom from Paul follow his warning about the dangers of immorality, but the basic principle can be applied to many areas. I contend that if people are diligent to discipline themselves in one area, it will contribute to doing the same in others. Besides, "flee also youthful lusts" (2 Timothy 2:22) requires running, and running requires being in shape, and being in shape requires discipline.

When I started riding motorcycles I had to be willing to strengthen my upper body. On several occasions I have had to call on some normally dormant muscles to keep my weighty, iron beast from laying down on the pavement. Being resolved to work on my physical body in order to accomplish this temporal goal is a good reminder to work on my "eternal temple" for the everlasting health benefits that can be enjoyed.

If you feel terribly undisciplined in your spiritual life at this moment, I encourage you to go buy a pair of tennis shoes and begin (slowly) an exercise regimen. You'll not only be amazed at how much better you'll feel in the flesh, but more importantly, you'll be surprised at the motivation you'll gain to train your spirit for the strengthening of your walk with Christ. That is a "little profit" worth experiencing!

Thank You, Father, for Your provision of this earthly body. I know it is a temple of Your Holy Spirit and a testimony to Your marvelous creative power. Help me make it fit for my journey with You. Help me make its very appearance a commentary on Your ability to help Your followers be a disciplined people. I don't want my out-of-shapeness to be a reproach on Your mighty capacity to change a life. I commit today to bring it under subjection and treat it like the divine gift that it is. In Jesus' name, amen.

> But I discipline my body and make it my slave,
> so that, after I have preached to others,
> I myself will not be disqualified.
>
> 1 Corinthians 9:27

36

The Man in Aisle 2

A wise son makes a father glad.

Proverbs 10:1

After my wife's mother died in 1996, her dad, who had been so close to his sweetheart for more than 52 years, found himself at a complete loss regarding how to take care of himself. For five decades N.R. had depended on Sylvia to help him remember to do important things like eat, dress appropriately for church, and curb his appetite for working to the point of exhaustion on their dairy farm.

The months that followed Sylvia's homegoing were excruciatingly painful for all the children, but not half as tough as it was for N.R. He tried to bravely conceal the emptiness he felt, but he couldn't do that very well. Because of their deep concern for their dad, his six children were careful to often be present in his home, to tend to their father's needs, and, most importantly, to provide company for him in a house that was once filled with the sound of his bride's voice but had now fallen eerily quiet. They were faithful to their dad until the day he went to be with the Lord in 1998.

Not every widower (or widow, for that matter) who experiences such a devastating loss was as blessed as Annie's dad was by his kids' care. For reasons ranging from extreme distances that cannot often be traversed to fathers having outlived their children, some men are left to fend for themselves. For whatever reason they are alone, the sight of an aged, nearly helpless widower is not always a pleasant thing to behold.

In an effort to remind those whose dads are in this situation and could use a timely visit from their kids, the following lyric was written.

Man in Aisle 2

Dear friend of mine, I write you this letter
How have you been since your mother passed away?
No one 'round here will ever forget her
And I need to tell you what I saw today

I saw your dad at the grocery this morning
He was wandering lost down aisle number two
We talked for a while, I said, "How've you been doing?"
He said he was fine but in his arms he held the truth

He had one TV dinner and a box of saltines
One shiny red apple and a can of beans
One small jar of coffee, the kind you make with a spoon
Dear friend of mine, are you coming home soon?

How quickly he said, "Yes!" when I invited him over
And he smiled when I said, "Supper time.
We'll set a place for three."
And as I was leaving I looked over my shoulder
And I wondered how you'd feel if you could see

That he had one TV dinner and a box of saltines
One shiny red apple and a can of beans
One small jar of coffee, the kind you make with a spoon
Dear friend of mine, are you coming home soon?[4]

Whether you are a son or a daughter, if this lyric describes the man you call your papa, perhaps a fair question to ask is, "When was the last time you went to see him?" If you're looking for a good excuse to head out on the open highway on your bike, maybe a ride to the old homeplace is just what the Divine Doctor is ordering for you right now. Maybe it will be the medicine you need to cure a case of homesickness. Or, better yet, it might even bring healing to two hearts that may have been severed at some point in the past. For whatever reason you have stayed away, has it been too long? Pack a few things and make the journey. And be sure to include in your saddlebags some fresh, ground coffee for brewing a pot that more than one can share.

Thank You, Father, for the way You gently remind me not to forget about the dads who are widowed and in need of someone to come and break the chains of loneliness. I pray for Your grace and strength and provision that I might make the journey to my dad's side. In Jesus' comforting name, amen.

Honor your father and your mother.

Exodus 20:12

37

"Matercycling"

*A man shall leave his father and his mother, and be joined
to his wife; and they shall become one flesh.*

Genesis 2:24

My heart is always warmed by the sight of a husband
and wife riding together on a motorcycle. When I behold
the scene, it tells me one or more of the following things:

- They are still good friends
- They both love cycling
- She trusts him
- He is grateful that she trusts him
- He feels guilty when he rides too much so he
  begged her to go along
- She's a good sport
- She thinks he's too handsome to go out in public
  alone
- He thinks she's too pretty to leave home without
  her
- She loves talking to him, even if it is through a
  helmet intercom system
- He loves talking to her while looking straight ahead
- He does better at talking while doing, which is why
  he's usually at the handlebars

- She probably has a few pipe burns to her credit
- He probably has a few claw marks on his neck
- More than likely they have good friends who bike
- They stop for coffee a lot
- They have children who worry about them
- They have children who try not to worry about
- She packs a lot lighter than a woman normally would
- He packs a lot heavier than a man normally would
- She knows how to lift his wallet without him knowing it
- He loves to control the radio (just like the TV remote at home)
- He has never gotten used to the tickling

What a great picture of the marriage union—two acting as one! I have a feeling you have your own list of pleasant thoughts that cross your mind when you see a couple biking together.

I want to mention one more thought: The most tender side of a man is brought out when he cycles with his wife. In fact, because of the inherent dangers that biking represents, he is more likely to live by Ephesians 5:28 while sharing the saddle with her as much as any other time: "So husbands ought also to love their own wives as their own bodies...."

No man I know wants to kiss the pavement, and, for sure, he carries that same fervor for his own safety into his role as a husband. Because his mate is so precious to him, she becomes his motivation to concentrate even more on the highway ahead. If he cares for his own hide so much, he's more than likely gonna care for hers. This is a very scriptural approach to biking…or "matercycling."

If your ride today includes you and your honey, may God bless you and reward you for being together. May the rest of your lives be just like your cycling—both of you going in the same direction. It's always a sweet sight to behold!

Thank You, Father, for the gift of my mate. As we journey together I pray that our hearts will continue to be molded together. I ask for Your mighty hand of protection as we move from one place to the next, both physically and spiritually. Help us show Your love to each other, a love that is unselfish and always mindful of the other person's needs. Until we see You face to face, Lord, be our guide. In Jesus' name, amen.

And the two shall become one flesh.

Ephesians 5:31

Two are better than one….

Ecclesiastes 4:9

38

Nothing Hidden

For My eyes are on all their ways;
they are not hidden from My face,
nor is their iniquity concealed from My eyes.

Jeremiah 16:17

Jim heard a noise on his back porch and went to check it out. Assuming that a stray dog might have been rummaging through the trashcans, he walked out onto the painted wooden surface of the rear deck to make sure that was what it was.

As Jim started down the back steps to take one last look around before getting out of the bitter cold, December night, he didn't see the ice that had engulfed the step. Suddenly, without warning, his legs went out from under him, and his head cracked on the corner of the top step.

The blood from the severe head wound poured onto the frozen grass. Jim did not regain consciousness. An hour passed, two hours, then three. Jim had bled profusely, but he died from exposure to the severe cold. Because he and his wife lived on a street where there was not much interaction between neighbors, the fences were high around the parameters of each home. Jim's wife had gone with some of her friends to a three-day women's conference. So no one could see his lifeless body as the frigid temperatures held on through the night and late into the next day.

As was her custom to touch base with Jim, his wife had tried to reach him by phone several times. She became quite concerned when he didn't answer. Fearing something was not right, she left the conference early. She was horrified when she discovered that her husband of 42 years had met with such a tragic end.

Jim had walked out his back door fully expecting to return a moment or two later to the warmth of his home. His appointment with death was a complete surprise. The TV was still on, the lights were still glowing, and the book he was reading had not been closed.

In the midst of the extreme sadness of this dark story, a ray of good light shone. Of all that remained of his life, one thing he did *not* leave behind was any evidence of sinful indulgences that he might have been trying to conceal. As his family went through his belongings, his chest of drawers, his workshop, his pickup, and his little fishing boat, they found no sign of shameful behavior. The only items found were some handwritten reminders of important things such as birth dates, anniversary gifts already bought to avoid duplication, doctor's scoldings about his heart condition that he didn't want to worry his wife with, and a few $2 bills he was saving for grandkids. Jim was squeaky clean.

When I heard how suddenly this gentle man had died and heard how pleased his family was with the assurance that he did his best to be righteous, I was inspired to strive for the same goal.

It would be smart of all of us to assume that at any given moment our "appointment" with eternity could come. With that in mind, it behooves us to ask: "Is there anything I am doing that I am trying to hide? What do I need to throw away? Is there a habit I should break at this moment and destroy the items that perpetuate it? What would my family find if I were to instantly go from this life to the next? What will I leave behind?"

Wouldn't the relieved sigh of your family members, who would find no sign of shame in your belongings, be worth whatever sin you need to give up? Imagine the added sadness that could be avoided if each of us lived like Jim did.

Far more valuable than having spouses and children who would be proud of a squeaky-clean life is the smile it brings to the face of our Father in heaven. The sobering truth is that He doesn't have to wait till we're gone to go through our "stuff." He sees it all right now. Whatever is hidden is not! Psalm 90:8 should make our hearts shudder in fear if we are attempting to conceal sin: "You have placed our iniquities before You, our secret sins in the light of Your presence."

Knowing that in one instant you might be here and the next you could be on your way to the presence of God, examine your heart. Is there anything not committed to the Lord? If so, yield that part of your life to Him now. And if there is something you've hidden that would bring reproach on your good name and that of the Savior's, in His strength, in His name, and to His glory, go straightway and destroy it—just in case you leave for heaven sooner than you think!

O Father in heaven, I am humbled by the thought that nothing is concealed from Your eyes. Help me live in such a way that if You call me quickly, my affairs will already be in order. I ask this so that You will receive the praise and honor due Your name. I want to be righteous before You and the people around me. In Jesus' name, amen.

Search me, O God, and know my heart; try me and know my anxious thoughts; and see if there be any hurtful way in me, and lead me in the everlasting way.

Psalm 139:23-24

Notes

1. "Will There Be Time?" Steve Chapman/Times & Seasons Music/BMI/© 1992. Used by permission.

2. "Sunday Morning Run," Steve Chapman/Times & Seasons Music/BMI/© 1989. Used by permission.

3. "Even When It Does Not Rain, He Reigns," Steve Chapman/Times & Seasons Music/BMI/© 2000. Used by permission.

4. "Man in Aisle 2," Steve Chapman/Times & Seasons Music/BMI/© 1997. Used by permission.

The Outdoor Insights
Pocket Book Series

Reel Time with God

With God on a Deer Hunt

With God on the Hiking Trail

With God on the Open Road